Contents

Welfare Services

A guide for care workers

Pat Young

School of Health and Social Studies
Colchester Institute

MACMILLAN

For Harry, Jake and Martin

First edition 1993
Reprinted 1994
Second edition 1997
Published by
MACMILLAN PRESS LTD
Houndmills, Basingstoke, Hampshire RG21 6XS
and London
Companies and representatives
throughout the world

ISBN 0–333–69954–8

A catalogue record for this book is available
from the British Library.

This book is printed on paper suitable for recycling and
made from fully managed and sustained forest sources.

10   9   8   7   6   5   4   3   2   1
06 05 04 03 02 01 00 99 98 97

Typeset by Wearset, Boldon, Tyne and Wear
Printed in Hong Kong

Acknowledgements

The author would like to thank those who helped at various stages in the preparation of this book, in particular Ruth Felstead, Terry Smyth, Emma Lee, Michael Key, David Tossell, Richard Webb and Arthur Baker who helped with the first edition; David Hicks who helped with this second edition.

The author and publishers wish to thank the following for providing their material for reproduction in the book: Age Concern England, page 27; Association of Community Health Councils for England & Wales, page 36, BACUP, page 35; Bristol Cancer Help Centre, page 66; British Dental Association, page 41; British Homeopathic Association, page 65; Cancer Relief Macmillan Fund, page 48; Cancerlink, page 33; Carers National Association/Sam Tanner, page 109; Centrepoint Soho, page 12; Cheltenham & Gloucester plc, page 22; Community Careline, Colchester, page 104 (top); Crown Copyright material, pages 8, 9, 10, 15, 16, 21, 29, 34, 39, 42, 55, 56, 77, 79, 84, 89, 92, 93, 99 (top), 112, 113, 132, 142, and 144; DaRT, page 100; Disabled Living Centres Council, page 107; Disabled Living Foundation, pages 98, 99 (foot) and 106; Family Planning Association, page 46; General Council and Register of Osteopaths, page 64; Peter Hayman and Lynda King (Rose Cottage Residential Home, Broughton, Cambs), page 134; Health Education Authority, page 51; Louis Hellman, page 97, Holiday Care Service, page 101; Independent Living 93 fund, page 86; National Childminding Association, page 128; Open University, page 117; Pre-School Learning Alliance/Margaret Hanton, page 130; Joseph Rountree Foundation – Family Fund, page 87; Shaftesbury House, page 11; SmithKline Beecham Consumer Healthcare, page 37; Society of Chiropodists, page 44; Suffolk County Council/Ipswich Social Services Department, page 104 (foot); Terrence Higgins Trust, page 50; Young Minds Trust, page 57.

1 About this book

The field of welfare is vast and complex. Many people are not aware of their rights and as a result do not get the best deal for themselves. The most vulnerable people often have the most difficulty in finding their way around the services, yet these are the very people who are likely to need the services most. Care workers can help by having enough knowledge to be able to assist their clients in finding out what their rights are and what services are available to them.

Recent trends in community care have increased the need for anyone working in care to have some knowledge of the welfare system. In the past, clients might have had all their needs met within one institution: now a complex package of care has to be put together by and for people living in the community. The package may include housing, income, health care, practical support, social activities and education or employment. The services involved are likely to include not just those within the welfare state, such as the National Health Service and social services, but also services provided by voluntary organisations and by the private sector. Community care also means that care workers have to function in a more independent way than before. A community psychiatric nurse, for example, will be part of a team of care workers, but she may well be the only person present when a client is distressed by a letter from her landlord giving her notice to quit.

Who is this book for?

The book will be helpful to you if you are already working in the care sector, if you are training for this kind of work, or if you are involved in caring in a more informal way – looking after a friend or relative, or as a volunteer worker.

- If you are employed as a full- or part-time worker in the health services, social services or with a voluntary organisation, you will find that it provides information which has a practical application in your work. You might use it while on an in-service training course.
- If you are preparing for assessment for a National Vocational Qualification (NVQ) or Scottish Vocational Qualification (SVQ), up to and including level 3, the book will help. It gives you the knowledge necessary to show competence in areas such as enabling clients to make use of available services and information, an important part of the effective care of clients.
- If you are a full- or part-time student taking, for example, a GNVQ, BTEC, City & Guilds or CCETSW qualification, you will find that this book includes information you need on social policy and welfare legislation. These courses usually include work experience: this book

will help you to develop your skills and understanding in a practical context.

- If you are following a training course leading to a professional qualification, in occupational therapy or social work, for example, you will find that the book gives a useful summary of welfare provision.

The aims of the book

The book aims to give information on welfare rights and welfare services, and to link this information into the practice of care. It is not expected that you will become an expert in all the fields described in the book – a kind of do-it-yourself lawyer *cum* social security adviser *cum* doctor! Rather you will gain the knowledge and understanding to be able to direct a client to a source of help and to give you confidence in supporting a client in dealing with the services.

The structure of the book

There are six chapters, covering the key areas of housing, health, money, daily living, employment and children.

The first chapter looks at ways to find help with housing and describes the legal position of tenants and owner-occupiers. There is a section on homelessness. The chapter on health is mainly concerned with the National Health Service, although alternative medicine and private health care are also covered. The work of voluntary organisations is considered, as for example in the case of provision for people with AIDS.

The chapter on money deals mostly with welfare benefits; while that on daily living looks at services providing practical care for people with disabilities, and sources of support and information. The chapter on employment looks at ways of finding work or training for work, as well as ways of becoming involved in voluntary work. The final chapter, on children, examines various types of daycare and covers the legislation protecting children.

Each chapter includes a variety of activities and practical work to help you put the information into the context of care in practice.

How to use this book

This is not a book to be read from cover to cover. The way you use it will depend on your own particular situation and the kind of care you are involved in. The book can be used as a reference source, in your workplace or when you are on a training course. You may want to dip into various chapters, perhaps to learn about a new area or to refresh your memory on something with which you are already familiar. You might be directed to particular sections or exercises as part of an educational or training course. Some of the activities will need to be discussed with a tutor or supervisor and shared with colleagues. They can be adapted to suit your own situation and needs.

Some of the activities and exercises involve finding out about people and organisations. It is a good idea to check with your supervisor or tutor before tackling these, to make sure that you approach the right person, and that you have permission – if necessary – to do so.

Many of the activities involve finding out information and reflecting on it. To make the best use of this information and your experiences you will find it useful to get into the habit of keeping a record of your learning. You will find the way which best suits your own purpose. If you have access to a computer or a word-processor, this may be the most convenient way to keep records of information and ideas. Other methods involve a note-book or loose-leaf file, or perhaps a card-index system for some kinds of information. Your supervisor or tutor will guide you.

Terms used

Care worker is used to describe people employed in caring or who are training for employment in caring. **Carer** is used to refer to someone who cares for a friend or relative. The 'carer' needs to know about the system every bit as much as the 'care worker'. **Client** is used throughout when describing the person being cared for, although those working in the health services may be more used to using the term 'patient'.

Keeping up to date

Although there is considerable continuity in care work and in social policy, there is also a process of continual change. Laws are revised and updated; benefits are modified to suit changing circumstances; policies and practices are adapted. Recently there have been some rather more fundamental changes, affecting the philosophy behind the provision of welfare.

I have dealt with the changes in policy in two ways: by indicating, where possible, the direction of change which seems likely in the future; and by giving ways of updating information.

Voluntary organisations

The book includes an appendix listing the addresses of organisations which may be able to provide more information. A lot of these are voluntary organisations, many of which work on shoestring budgets. Although these organisations will usually welcome enquiries, you should always send a stamped addressed envelope when you write for information, and be prepared to pay for leaflets and booklets.

2 Housing

Housing problems cut into all aspects of life. At the extreme there is the growing problem of homelessness. Without a home it is difficult to get and hold down a job. Homeless people cannot enjoy stable relationships or possessions. Even in temporary housing, such as bed and breakfast, the quality of family life is affected. Anxieties about the security and safety of housing also affect people's lives. Homelessness and worries about housing can be a cause of both physical and mental health problems.

People who are homeless or worried about losing their home need help and advice. There are many decisions to be made. There are agencies and people who can help; but a client may need advice about where to turn, and guidance and support through the maze of choices.

Problems to do with housing affect people in many varying situations. Each client is different and will be treated as such. The kind of advice and support offered will depend on the nature of your relationship to the client. Nurses in the fields of mental health and learning disability help patients in transitions from hospital to the community. Housing is a key issue in a successful move to independent living. Young people leaving the care of the local authority need the support of residential and other social workers in making this move. Older people living on their own in the community may need to find a more sheltered form of housing and may seek the advice and support of their carers.

This chapter explains the various sources of advice and information on housing. You may use these yourself or refer a client to them. You may accompany a client on a visit; asking for help, especially when stressed, can be difficult. The chapter also explains, in outline, some aspects of the law on housing. You will not be competent to give legal advice, but at least you should know what rights people have. A client can then be advised to seek proper legal help.

2.1 Housing advice and information

There are several sources of advice and information on housing problems. The ones described below should be available in most areas. There will also be services which are special to one local area.

Housing advice centres

Most towns have a **housing advice centre** (or 'housing aid centre'). These are run by the local council, but do not help only council tenants: they offer advice and information to all local people. The help is free. Housing advice centres can help with most kinds of housing problems, including homelessness, difficulties with rent, abuse by landlords, noise and other environmental issues, threatened repossession of a home and domestic violence. The office is usually to be found in the town centre, perhaps in a converted shop.

Housing advice centres have information leaflets. They give personal advice on individual problems. They will also contact other parts of the council, or other organisations such as the Department of Social Security. In some cases they are able to represent clients in legal arguments with landlords or building societies.

Lists of housing advice centres can be obtained from Shelter London, for the London area, and from the Resource Information Service for other parts of the country.

Citizens' Advice Bureaux (CAB)

All parts of the UK have **Citizens' Advice Bureaux**. They can offer general advice and information on housing (as well as on many other matters). If more detailed advice is needed, the CAB will know where to go to find it. Many bureaux provide free appointments with a solicitor, usually one evening a week.

Solicitors

Names and addresses of solicitors can be found in *Yellow Pages*. Other organisations such as housing advice centres can also provide lists of solicitors, usually saying which offer **legal aid**. Solicitors provide legal advice. If someone is on benefits or has a low income, he or she will be entitled to legal aid, which means that the services of the solicitor will be free. Even if the person is not entitled to legal aid, many solicitors offer a fixed fee appointment. This means that they will give up to half an hour's advice for £5.00. Sometimes a preliminary interview will be given free.

Local newspapers

Local newspapers have advertisements of places to rent and to buy. Libraries keep copies of these newspapers, which can be read by anyone, free.

Helplines

The Housing Advice Line, run by Shelter, gives advice and information on any aspect of housing.

Finding out more: housing

★ More general information on housing issues can be found from **Shelter**. Shelter is a voluntary organisation which campaigns for homeless people. It publishes many excellent leaflets and books. A list of these can be obtained by writing to Shelter.

★ The Resource Information Service publishes practical information on dealing with homelessness.

★ The Children Act Housing Group publishes *In on the Act* which helps people working with homeless single people and also a guide to benefits for homeless single people. The Children Act Working Group is based at CHAR.

2.2 Finding a home – types of housing

This section covers the various types of housing available. The choice will depend on the amount of money the client has, as well as other factors such as the availability of the different sorts of housing in the local area. The most obvious ways to get a home are to buy or to rent. Most people who buy do so with a mortgage from a bank or building society, but this is not the only way. Houses can be rented from private owners or from the council. In the rented sector there are also housing associations, which are a good source of reasonably priced housing. This section looks at these ways of finding housing, as well as housing co-operatives, shared-ownership schemes, and finding accommodation in hostels and nightshelters.

Buying a house

Some people buy their house outright. Most, though, have to borrow money for such an expensive purchase. **Mortgages** to buy a house can be sought from building societies, banks or the local authority. Finance companies will also lend money for housing, but they are not recommended as interest rates are higher. They are also less likely to be sympathetic if the person cannot meet the mortgage repayments.

Lenders vary as regards how much they are prepared to lend. The amount depends also on a number of other factors, to do with the circumstances of the borrower and the type of property to be bought. As a rough guide, someone could expect to borrow two-and-a-half to three times their gross income. It is common for lenders to ask for a deposit of between five and ten per cent of the value of the property although it is possible to get 100 per cent mortgages.

In some cases, for instance after a house has been repossessed by a building society or bank or where the income seems very insecure, it may be necessary to have a **guarantor** for a mortgage. The guarantor is someone who agrees to be responsible for the mortgage if the payments are not made. Local authorities can take this role – either through the 1985 Housing Act, or through social services. Social services can help if there is a child in the family and buying a house will prevent the family from becoming homeless.

Some property developers offer **rental purchase agreement** schemes which commit a tenant to buy a property at a later date. The details should be carefully checked by a legal adviser and no one should enter such a scheme without being sure they are able to meet all future payments and that they would qualify for a mortgage if they are expected to arrange one.

The 'right to buy'

The 1980 Housing Act brought in the right for council tenants to buy their homes. This right applies after two years and most homes are eligible, but not sheltered housing. Tenants get a discount on the price – 32 per cent after two years, rising to 60 per cent after 30 years. The discount on flats is higher, starting at 44 per cent and rising to 70 per cent. If the house is sold within three years, part of the discount must be repaid.

Tenants wishing to buy are also entitled to a mortgage. This can be up to 100 per cent of the loan. The income on which the calculation is based can include several members of a family, such as two parents and a grown-up and working son or daughter who also lives there. If the council does not provide the loan itself, it will arrange for a building society to provide it.

There is also a Rent-to-Mortgage Scheme which allows people to buy their council house by paying only part of the price at the beginning. An initial payment is calculated on the basis of how much rent is being paid. In most cases a mortgage is obtained to make this payment and the mortgage payments are therefore more or less the same as the rent. The rest of the price can be paid at the end of the period of paying off the initial payment. Alternatively, part of the price can again be paid. If the house is sold, the landlord receives a share of the current value of the house, for example one third in a situation where the initial payment was two thirds.

The 1996 Housing Bill extends the 'right to buy' to tenants of new housing association properties. Discounts will range from £8000 to £26 000, depending on the area of the country. There is also a voluntary scheme for tenants of existing housing association properties.

The 'right to buy'

Shared ownership

Many people will find that their income is too low to allow them to borrow enough money to buy even the smallest house. **Shared ownership** schemes are a way of helping less well-off people to buy a home. Most are operated by local authorities or by housing associations. The ownership of the property is shared between the individual occupier and the organisation. The occupier pays off a mortgage in the usual way on his or her own share of the property, and also pays rent on the remainder. The occupier's share of the ownership can be increased as time goes on.

Housing co-operatives

A **housing co-operative** is a group of people who manage and control the housing they live in. Everyone is equal in the co-op and no one individually owns the property or makes money out of anyone else. Everyone pays a fair share of the costs. Usually the property is collectively owned by the co-op, although there are also management co-ops. In such cases, the property is owned by a council or housing association, but all the day-to-day running of the housing is managed by the co-op. Grants are available towards the cost of establishing a co-op: these are provided by the government, through the housing corporation.

Housing co-ops have many benefits. They are a means of achieving decent housing. They are a way of avoiding the 'red tape' of council housing. They give people power over their own homes, with shared responsibility. A housing co-op often gives a much greater sense of community to the residents than any other kind of housing. However, co-ops also involve the hard work of co-operating with others over the management of the housing. This involves a certain amount of commitment.

Privately rented housing

This is perhaps the simplest way of finding somewhere to live. It suits people who do not want the ties of owning a house. It is however an expensive option, and gives the occupant few rights over his or her housing. A lot of the people who rent privately do so because they cannot find anything better. Rented property can be found through an agency, or through local newspapers. Agencies can be expensive and in some cases are prepared to manage accommodation which fails to meet safety standards. In some areas accommodation projects have been established to help young people find accommodation in rooms, bedsits or hotels. Shop noticeboards also often have advertisements of rooms to rent. Housing Benefit can be claimed by tenants on a low income or certain benefits (see Chapter 4). A later section in this chapter describes the rights and duties both of landlords or landladies and of tenants.

Council housing

It is increasingly difficult to get a council house or flat. Councils have lost a lot of property as a result of having to sell houses to tenants. In deciding who to house, councils operate a **points system**. People who apply to the council are allocated a certain number of points, depending on their circumstances, their needs and their present housing. The number of points determines where the person is placed on the waiting list. This in turn decides how quickly, if ever, the person will be offered a house or a flat. A single childless person in good health, for example, has very little chance of being housed.

Tenants of the council have rights, under the 1980 Housing Act. They have **security of tenure** (they cannot be evicted without there being certain reasons and procedures); they have the right to sub-let and to improve the property; and they have the right to receive certain information. After two years, tenants have the right to buy their home (see earlier). Tenants can swap council houses, and there is a national computerised scheme to help people to contact each other.

There is a Council Tenant's Charter which sets out a series of rights for council tenants as well as describing the responsibilities of the council. For example, the council is required to maintain the structure and exterior of the home as well as the basins, sinks, baths and toilets, central heating and water heaters. Tenants are entitled to compensation if repairs are not

Shared ownership schemes make buying a home cheaper

carried out. Tenants are allowed to carry out their own improvements, with permission from the council, and have a right to compensation for improvements.

The 1988 Housing Act brought in a scheme whereby tenants can vote to have a different landlord. There is also provision under this Act for trusts to be set up by the government to take over the most run-down estates. These trusts are called **Housing Action Trusts (HATs)**. The intention was that they would improve the estate over a period of five years and then pass it on to a new landlord.

Housing associations

There are about half a million flats and houses owned and rented out by housing associations in Britain. A **housing association** is a non-profit-making organisation which aims to provide good-quality housing at a reasonable rent for people who might not otherwise find such housing. Some housing associations are small and locally based; others are larger. They offer various sorts of housing, including flats and houses and also sheltered housing and hostel-type schemes. Some properties are newly built; some are converted and renovated. Many housing associations help people with special needs, such as people with disabilities. Others focus on the housing needs of young people.

There are various ways in which people get into housing-association property. Some people are nominated by the council: this is the case for about 50 per cent of housing-association tenants. Sometimes housing advice centres can nominate tenants. Some housing associations have

The Council Tenant's Charter sets out council tenants' rights

TO DO

Have a look at the Council Tenant's Charter. There should be a copy in the local library and in the Council Offices. Alternatively, you can write to The Council Tenant's Charter to obtain your own copy (the address is in the appendix).

Living in a housing association home

waiting lists. The housing association will interview people applying and will usually make its decision on the basis of need.

The 1988 Housing Act brought in a Tenants' Guarantee which means that certain rights must be included in all housing association tenancy agreements. Tenants with a complaint about a housing association can go to the Housing Association Tenants' Ombudsman Service (address in the appendix of this book). Information leaflets and advice on how to make a complaint are also available.

Hostels and nightshelters

Most towns have various **hostels**. These range from Women's Aid houses, for women who have suffered violence from their partners, to hostels run by the social services departments for people with psychiatric problems. Some hostels are run by voluntary organisations, some by the local authority, and some by private organisations. They are usually for people with special needs of some kind. Some are for young people who find themselves homeless. Hostels usually offer rooms to rent and many provide support and guidance as well as shelter. As with everything else, the facilities and support offered vary in quality and there are some hostels where profits are prioritised above providing a sympathetic understanding of vulnerable people's needs.

Nightshelters provide temporary accommodation for homeless people. They are usually run by voluntary organisations. Often the shelter is limited by age and sex. Some shelters are specifically for young people; others will not accept people under a certain age. The shelters usually offer washing and laundry facilities. The staff are accepting and sympathetic, although basic rules, such as a ban on alcohol and drugs, are strictly followed.

Reception at a shelter for young people in London

WORDCHECK

housing advice centre A centre that offers free advice on all aspects of housing.

legal aid A scheme under which people with a low income can receive free advice from a solicitor.

voluntary organisation An organisation which has not been set up by the government and which does not aim to make a profit.

mortgage A loan to buy a house: the house is used as security on the loan and can therefore be repossessed if the loan is not paid.

housing association A voluntary organisation which provides housing for rent.

housing co-operative A group of people managing their own housing collectively.

shared ownership A scheme which allows people to buy part of a house or flat and to rent the other part.

guarantor A person who takes responsibility for someone else's loan.

Council Tenant's Charter A charter setting out the responsibilities of the council to its tenants and the rights of the tenants.

nightshelter A centre that provides very basic overnight accommodation for homeless people.

Housing Benefit A benefit to help with the costs of rent, for people on a low income.

points system A system used by local councils in allocating housing.

Housing Action Trusts (HATs) Trusts set up by the government to take over run-down council estates.

security of tenure The right of a tenant to remain in his or her home.

TO DO

Select three of your clients. Consider their housing needs. Make a list of all the forms of housing available to each client.

- What would be the advantages and disadvantages of each type of housing?
- How would you advise the client to find out details of each type of housing?

(If you work with older people, you may wish to read the final section of this chapter before doing this exercise.)

Finding out more: buying a house

★ The Department of the Environment publishes an attractive and readable booklet which is a guide to buying a council house or flat. It is called *Your Right to Buy Your House*, and is available from the local council or CAB. Another Department of the Environment leaflet describes the Rent-to-Mortgage Scheme. Both leaflets can also be obtained by writing to the Department of the Environment at the address listed in the appendix.

★ There are several types of housing co-operatives. These are described, along with other details, in a leaflet called *Housing Co-operatives*, produced by the Housing Corporation.

★ The Housing Corporation also offers a leaflet called *Shared Ownership*.

Finding out more: self-build schemes

★ Another way into home-ownership is with self-build schemes. The Housing Corporation publishes a leaflet which explains how these work and what help is available. Information is also available from The Community Self-Build Agency, and from the National Federation for Housing Associations.

2.3 Tenants' rights

This section looks at the law which relates to renting a home. Some people choose to rent: perhaps they do not want the responsibility of owning a house; perhaps they are renting temporarily – because of a short-term job, or before deciding to buy. Many people, however, rent from a private owner because they have no choice. There are many reasons for this. One is that council houses are becoming harder to find, as more and more are sold off to existing tenants. Another is that not everyone qualifies for a mortgage to buy a house: a certain level of secure income is needed. Young people leaving the care of the local authority are unlikely to be able to buy a house, unless they have a very well paid job. They would not qualify for council housing without children, unless in poor health or perhaps under a special scheme for young people. Older people who have been used to renting may continue to rent, as this was more popular in the past. People leaving institutions such as psychiatric hospitals or hospitals for those with mental disabilities are unlikely to be in a position to buy. There may be special schemes provided by the health authority, by the social services or by a voluntary organisation, but often these are inadequate to meet the need. Care workers are likely to be involved with people who are renting.

It is useful for care workers to know something of the rights which tenants have under the law. Many tenants do not know their rights, or how to make use of their rights. Support and advice may be needed, especially by vulnerable people such as those with learning difficulties. By knowing something of the law, it is possible that you could help to prevent someone from becoming homeless. And this in itself could avert a number of other problems.

The rights considered here fall into three main areas. Firstly there is the law concerning **security of tenure** – in other words, the tenant's right to stay in his or her home and the rights of the owner to evict a tenant. This is perhaps the most important area, but also the most complicated. The second area concerns rent. There are some laws about the amounts of rent which can be charged by an owner. The final area concerns repairs to the property – the obligations both of the owner and of the tenant.

Housing law is complicated. This is mainly because successive governments have passed a number of different Acts over the years. Some of these have given tenants more rights: some have substantially reduced their rights. When a new law comes in, it affects new tenancies from a particular date. People already renting their home continue to be under the old law and have the old rights. More recent laws have taken away some tenants' rights, so people who begin to rent a house now will probably have fewer rights than those who have been renting for a long time. An important date in this is 15 January 1989, since this is when the 1988 Housing Act came into effect.

Evictions

Tenancies created before 15 January 1989

Most tenancies where the tenant moved in before 15 January 1989 are Rent Act-protected tenancies. It is harder for an owner to get a tenant out of these tenancies than from a more recent letting.

Two things must happen before a tenant can be evicted:

● A tenant must be given a **notice to quit**. This is a formal document which must allow at least four weeks' notice and which must tell the tenant that legal advice is available. It might be a good idea for a solicitor to check whether the document has been compiled properly; if not, it is not legally binding. In any case, it is important to realise that a notice to quit does not mean the tenant must leave.

● The owner must get a **possession order** from the court. This is only given if certain grounds, or reasons, can be proven.

There are six situations in which the court will always give the property back to the owner, regardless of the effect on the tenant. One example of these is when an owner-occupier wants to move back into the house. Another is where the property is classed as either a holiday let or a shorthold tenancy.

There are also discretionary grounds for eviction. In these cases the court will take account of the *reasonableness* of the decision. It would look, for example, at the behaviour of the owner and of the tenant, and also at the needs of each. If the tenant had children, the effects of eviction on the children would be taken into account. Examples of these grounds are:

● not paying the rent;
● sub-letting;
● keeping pets when this is not allowed;
● annoying the neighbours, for example with late-night parties.

There are also reasons to do with the **convenience** to the owner. In other words the court will consider whether the owner has a good reason for wanting the property back. Examples of these are:

● the tenant was employed by the owner and now the owner needs the property for a new worker;
● the tenant earlier gave notice that he or she was going to leave and the owner made arrangements for a new tenant to move in.

Tenancies created after 15 January 1989

In 1988 a new Housing Act was passed. The government wanted to make more houses available to rent. It believed that people were put off from renting houses out because they were worried that tenants could not be evicted. So the new law makes it easier for owners to get tenants out. Another important change concerned rents; this is considered on page 17.

The new tenancies are called **assured tenancies**. To repossess the house the owner must still get a court order, but no notice to quit is required. The owner serves a notice that he or she intends to repossess the house, and tells the tenant the reason. If the reason concerns something the tenant has done wrong, court proceedings can start after two weeks. In other cases the owner must wait for two months.

A solicitor can help with a housing problem

Tenants can be evicted if they break the rules of the tenancy

The grounds for repossession of assured tenancies are similar to those for protected tenancies, but they are more generous to the owner. In some cases the owner must let the tenant know from the beginning that the property may be repossessed. The grounds where this is the case include the following:

● the owner lived in the house before it was rented out: no reason for wanting the house back needs to be given;
● the owner has a mortgage on the house which he or she cannot pay, and the house cannot be sold with tenants living in it.

With the following reasons, the tenant does not have to be warned at the beginning of the tenancy:

● the owner needs to do major repairs which cannot be done with the tenant living there, or the owner wants to knock the house down;
● at least three weeks' rent has not been paid.

The *discretionary* grounds – where the court will examine the situation of the owner and the tenant – include cases in which the tenant:

● owes rent;
● has often delayed in paying the rent;
● has not looked after the property.

The law also allows for short-term lets. These are called **assured shorthold tenancies**. With a shorthold tenancy it is agreed at the beginning that the tenancy will be for a fixed period of time (at least six months). Unless the tenant or the owner breaks the agreed rules of the contract in some way, neither can end the tenancy before the time is up.

In all of the situations described above it would be a good idea for a tenant who is threatened with an eviction to consult a solicitor. This should be done as soon as possible.

A final point worth mentioning here is that social services departments can make payments to prevent children from coming into care. Although social services do not have much money available, the 1989 Children Act allows funds to be used in this way.

TO DO

1 Arrange to visit the local court on a day when repossession hearings are being heard. These are heard in the county court and the telephone number is listed in the *Yellow Pages*, under 'Courts'.

2 Listen to a number of cases. Notice what the court is taking note of.

Courts can be intimidating places – even when you're not being accused of anything – so you might want to do this exercise with a colleague. Also bear in mind that you are not allowed to take notes in court.

Rents

Again the situation regarding rents varies according to the type of tenancy.

Tenancies created before 15 January 1989

These are **protected tenancies**, under the 1977 Rent Act. With this type of tenancy, a fair rent can be set. The fair rent is decided by the rent officer, an employee of the local council. Either the owner or the tenant can apply for a **fair rent** to be set; this rent will then be registered. The decision about the amount of rent is made on the basis of the property – the size, condition, and so on. The decision is not influenced by the scarcity of places to rent. In other words a high rent will not be set just because there is nowhere else to live and people are so desperate they will pay any amount to have a home.

Tenancies created after 15 January 1989

These are **assured tenancies**, under the 1988 Housing Act. At the beginning of the tenancy, the owner is entirely free to set any rent he or she likes. The only control applies to rent increases *after* the tenant has moved into the property. After a year the owner can raise the rent. If the tenant is not happy about this, he or she can go to the **Rent Assessment Committee**. They will assess the rent, on the basis of the current rent if the house or flat was to be re-let – in other words, the Rent Assessment Committee will try to set the current market value.

With an **assured shorthold tenancy** the tenant does not have to wait for the owner to increase the rent. He or she can go immediately to the Rent Assessment Committee who will decide what the market rent should be.

Repairs

The owner has a responsibility to keep the basic structure of the house or flat in good repair. The owner's duties include the upkeep of:

- drains, gutters and pipes;
- the supply of gas, electricity and water;
- heating systems and water heating;
- toilets, sinks, baths and showers.

The owner does not have to make repairs if the damage has been done by the tenant, however. Decorating inside is the responsibility of the tenant. And it is up to the tenant to report any repairs that need doing, and then to allow the owner access to inspect and to make repairs.

If the owner does not keep the property in good condition, he or she can be sued in court. Another way is to involve the council. The environmental health department of the council will prosecute an owner whose property is a danger to health. The council can require an owner to make a property fit for habitation. If the owner ignores this, the council can do the work itself and get the money back from the owner.

WORDCHECK

security of tenure The right of a tenant to remain in his or her home.

notice to quit A formal document which tells a tenant that the owner intends to take back the property.

possession order A document from the court granting the right to repossess a home.

protected tenancy An older type of tenancy which gives the tenants more rights than other types.

assured tenancy A relatively new kind of rented property from which the tenant can more easily be evicted.

shorthold tenancy A tenancy agreement for a short term only.

fair rent Rent set on a protected tenancy by the local rent officer.

Finding out more: tenants and the law

★   For a more detailed explanation of the law relating to rented property, see Hugh Brayne and Gerry Martin's *Law for Social Workers* (Blackstone Press: fourth edition, 1995).

★   Another source is *The Which? Guide to Renting and Letting* by Peter Wilde (Which? Ltd: second edition, 1995).

TO THINK ABOUT

What rights would the people in the following situations have?

(a) A family who are renting a house are troubled by a seriously leaking roof.

(b) A man has recently moved into a flat, with an agreed rent of £200 a month. As soon as he had settled in, the owner raised the rent to £300.

TO DO

Consider any clients you have who live in rented property, and try to find out something about their situations.

● What kind of tenancies do they have?

● What rights do they have? In what circumstances could they be evicted?

2.4 Problems with mortgages

More and more people are buying houses with loans from banks or building societies. This is partly because it has become harder to find homes to rent – as more council houses are sold off and fewer places are available to rent privately. But it is also because government policies have encouraged people to buy. Council-house rents have increased. Tenants of private owners have fewer and fewer rights. Many people have bought council houses, with very generous discounts and 100 per cent mortgages.

Many people have benefited from buying their own home. But as the number of owners has increased, so too has the number of people experiencing problems in repaying mortgages. In earlier days owner-occupation was an option taken up by better-off people with secure jobs. It was very rare for people to default on their mortgages and for the building society to repossess the house. Now the extension of owner-occupation to less well-off people has changed things. It is becoming increasingly common for banks and building societies to repossess houses.

Unemployment is often the reason people can no longer pay their mortgage. As unemployment rises, so do repossessions. Unemployment has hit hard in recent years – even in areas of work where people thought they were safe. Another common cause of mortgage **arrears** is separation and divorce. Often the woman is left in the house but is unable to go on paying the mortgage.

Meeting mortgage payments

People who are unemployed may be entitled to help with the cost of a mortgage on the house they live in. This covers the interest on the mortgage, not the capital repayments, and does not apply if the loan was taken out while the person was on benefit or during a period of 26 weeks between two benefit claims. There are also restrictions on the amounts paid for very high mortgages.

Help with the mortgage is not given straight away when someone claims benefit. It is expected that people will have mortgage protection insurance or savings to cover them for the initial period of unemployment. People over 60, however, do get immediate help. The periods of time vary due to a change in the rules in 1995:

- Loans taken out before 2 October 1995:
  - Nothing for the first 8 weeks on benefit
  - 50% of mortgage interest for the next 18 weeks
  - full mortgage interest after 26 weeks;
- Loans taken out after 1 October 1995:
  - nothing for the first 39 weeks of benefit
  - full mortgage interest after 39 weeks.

Losing a home

This section explains what happens if someone cannot meet his or her mortgage repayments. It also describes the best strategy for people wishing to keep their home. Although some people decide to give up their home – finding the worry of trying to meet mortgage repayments too much to cope with – there are disadvantages to this course of action. The most obvious is that the person loses the home and may not find it easy to find another. The council may consider people to be 'intentionally homeless' if they have voluntarily given back a home they owned. In this case the council do not have to provide permanent accommodation. A drop in house prices may mean that the house is sold for less than the buying price, leaving the owner in debt to the building society or bank. When building societies sell houses, they do not always get the best deal possible and money may be lost in this way. Finally, someone who has had a house repossessed may find it difficult to get any kind of credit afterwards and hard to get another mortgage at a later date.

Stages of repossession

If the repayments on a mortgage are not made, the lender – the bank, the building society or whatever – is entitled to apply to the court to evict the owner. The house will then be sold to pay off the loan. Any money left over will go to the owner. For this to happen, a number of procedures have to be followed. Note, however, that *the process can be stopped at any time.*

Stage 1
When repayments stop, the building society will write, asking that the payments be brought up to date.

Stage 2
The building society will write again, threatening legal action.

Stage 3
The building society will pass details to its solicitors. The solicitors will contact the court.

Stage 4
The court will issue a **summons**. This will give a date for the hearing.

Stage 5
The court hearing. A number of options are possible:

- Arrears are paid: no possession order is issued.
- Arrears to be paid in the future: a *suspended* possession order is issued.
- A possession order is issued. This sets a date, usually within 28 days, for repossession.

Stage 6
On the day set, the lender applies for a **possession warrant**. The court gives details to its officials – the **bailiffs** – who decide a date and time. They inform the owner-occupier.

Stage 7
If the house is still occupied when the bailiffs arrive, they will evict the owner.

Avoiding repossession

There are various things which owner-occupiers can do if they are having difficulty in paying the mortgage. The ideal time to take action is at the

Get in touch with the building society

very beginning. It is best not to stop paying the mortgage, even if the full amount cannot be paid. The owner should get in touch with the building society or bank. It may be able to help by *rearranging* the mortgage. Building societies do not want to evict people and repossess homes. It is trouble for them. And they can be quite flexible in making decisions. If a mortgage has been organised to include payment of arrears, it is important to keep making payments. Each time a repayment is missed, it takes far longer for the arrears to be paid off.

The details of how mortgages can be rearranged depend on the type of mortgage involved. A **capital repayment mortgage** works in a different way from an **endowment mortgage**. With a capital repayment mortgage, two courses of action are possible:

- to pay the interest only, for a period of time;
- to make a new mortgage arrangement over a longer period of time – this would mean lower monthly payments.

An endowment mortgage is less flexible. For this reason it may be best to swap to a capital repayment mortgage. (This may also turn out to be cheaper.) As an alternative, it may be possible to stop paying the policy premiums for a short period of time. It is unlikely that this could continue for more than six months.

Once the lender has started the procedure of repossessing the house, it is still possible to stop the process. Although this can be done at any stage, it is important not to delay. If the bank or building society is sending threatening letters, but has not yet applied for a court hearing, the owner should contact the bank or building society. An offer should be made to clear the arrears and a promise made concerning future payments. As described above, the building society can be asked to help in reducing the payments.

After the court summons has arrived, it is possible to ask for an **adjournment**. This will allow time to work out a plan. The best way is to write to the building society's solicitors to ask them to agree to delay whilst negotiations take place. If they refuse, it is still possible for the court to agree to an adjournment. It is possible to ask the court to allow an adjournment at the actual hearing. Since it may not agree, though, the owner should be prepared to present his or her case anyway.

Even when a possession order or warrant has been made, it is possible for the court to prevent an eviction. New proposals can be offered at a further hearing.

Paying arrears

In order to keep the house, the owner must show how the arrears can be paid off.

- This can be done with a lump sum, or arrangements can be made for gradual repayments over a set period of time. If the person is on Income Support, the interest payments and an amount towards the arrears can be deducted from the benefit and paid directly to the lender.
- Social services have the power to give money if by doing so a child could be prevented from coming into care. Although social services do not have a very big budget, this money can be used to prevent a family becoming homeless, if homelessness might mean a child coming into care.
- There are a number of charities which can give grants for particular purposes. Most libraries have a copy of *The Directory of Grant-Making Trusts*, which lists and briefly describes these charities.
- The building society may be persuaded to add the arrears to the capital already owed. This money can then be repaid through increased monthly repayments.

Negative equity

Many people have been affected by falls in property prices. For some people this has created a situation in which the house or flat is valued at less than the amount of money left to pay on the mortgage. This creates a problem for people wanting to move. Building societies have devised Negative Equity Mortgage Schemes to help people in this situation. These schemes allow people to buy another house, transferring the negative equity amount to the new mortgage.

Leases

People who have bought flats with long leases are entitled to have the lease extended or to buy the lease collectively with other people living in the flats.

Finding out more: problems with mortgages

★   Shelter publishes an excellent book of advice for home-owners. As well as explaining in more detail what to do if there are problems with mortgage repayments, it covers ways of increasing income by claiming

C&G Negative Equity Mortgage

Now negative equity needn't stop you moving

C&G
Cheltenham & Gloucester

Building societies can help people with negative equity who want to move house

TO DO

Find a copy of *The Directory of Grant-Making Trusts*, which is probably available in your local library. Look at the range of organisations involved, and the purposes for which they offer grants. Are there any charities which could be useful to any of your clients?

benefits and other measures. It is regularly updated, and published in association with the Child Poverty Action Group. The title is *Rights Guide for Home-Owners*. It is available from Shelter.

WORDCHECK

possession order A document from the court granting the right to repossess a home.

arrears Money owed.

capital repayment mortgage A type of mortgage whereby the borrower pays back monthly sums which consist of interest and the loan itself.

endowment mortgage A type of mortgage in which the capital of the loan is paid off at the end of the period through an insurance policy.

summons A letter from the court informing the recipient of the date of a hearing.

bailiffs Representatives of the court, who have power to enforce a possession order.

adjournment An agreement by the court to delay proceedings until a later date.

negative equity a problem faced by owner-occupiers when the value of their house falls below the amount of money owed on a mortgage.

2.5 Homelessness

People can become homeless for many reasons. Newspapers and television cameras have shown the increasing numbers of young people who sleep rough on the streets of London and other towns in Britain. Some of these people have run away from sexual and other forms of abuse at home. Some have been thrown out by their parents or step-parents. Until they are 18 it is difficult for them to claim any money from social security (see Chapter 4 for details). A high proportion of young homeless people have been in the care of social services and have no parental home. Others cannot go home because their parents have divorced and remarried, and will no longer house them.

About one in eight people who become homeless have had to leave a room, flat or house they have been renting. People who rent their home have no right to stay on after the agreement ends, even if they have nowhere else to go (see section 2.3).

The fastest-growing kind of homelessness is where people can no longer pay a mortgage and the house is taken back by the lender. The rise in interest rates has made it harder for people to pay their mortgages. Unemployment too can mean the loss of a home. (See section 2.4 for advice on what to do when a mortgage cannot be paid.)

Homelessness and the law

The borough or district council has certain duties towards homeless people. To qualify for help from the council the person must have no accommodation in which they are entitled to live, or be threatened with homelessness in the next 28 days. A woman would be seen as homeless if she cannot live with her husband because he is violent.

The local authority will provide temporary housing for 12 months for people in the following situations:

- when there are children in the family;
- when the homeless person is older, mentally ill, has a disability, or is seen as vulnerable for some other reason;
- when homelessness is caused by a fire, flood or other emergency.

The 12 month period can be extended.

In considering whether to help a homeless person, the council must decide if the person's homelessness is intentional. In other words, did the person do something which made him or her homeless? **Intentional homelessness** would include somebody who did not manage his or her money very well, who got into arrears with the rent, and who was evicted as a result. The homeless person can apply to the court for a review if he or she does not agree with what the court says.

The council will also consider whether the person has a 'local connection' with another local authority, in which case the problem will be passed on to that area.

The temporary housing provided will not necessarily be in council-owned property but could be with a private landlord or a hostel run by a voluntary organisation. Permanent housing in a council flat or house or a housing association property is allocated through the waiting list where the needs of homeless people are considered along with those of others on the list.

CASE STUDIES

Imagine that the following people are clients of yours. What would you advise? What options are available, and what are the advantages and disadvantages of each?

(a) Debbie is 16. She is desperately unhappy at home since her mother remarried. She tells you she wants to move out.

(b) Mandy and Leon have been married for one year. They each had a well-paid job and so they were able to buy an expensive flat. Now Mandy is pregnant and wants to give up her job, and yesterday Leon's firm made him redundant.

(c) Ted has mild learning disabilities. For several years he has been a lodger in a house belonging to Mrs Nash, a widow aged 70. Her relatives have now suggested that she move in with them and sell her own house. Mrs Nash has agreed to do this, but is concerned about Ted.

TO FIND OUT

What happens to homeless people in your area? The local authority housing department should be able to help you to answer these questions:

- How many homeless people are known to the housing department?
- What accommodation does the council use to house homeless people?
- How long do people usually have to stay in temporary accommodation?

WORDCHECK

local authority The local council, which in the case of housing could be a borough or district council.

intentional homelessness Homelessness deliberately caused by the client: the legislation on homelessness gives the local authority different and lesser duties in such cases.

2.6 Older people – special housing needs

Many of the people helped by the caring professions are older people. They mostly live in their own homes in the community. They may have the support and help of social workers, home helps, district nurses and other community carers.

Older people often have special housing needs. The houses they live in are more likely to be old and in poor condition. Older people sometimes live in houses originally bought for a young family, which are not suited to the needs of an older person living alone. Sometimes an older person may become too frail to live alone. Some older people feel very insecure on their own, and feel the need to know that help is closer to hand. This section considers the possibilities open to older people who need more care than is provided in ordinary housing.

Sheltered housing

Sheltered housing has become increasingly popular. It meets the needs of people who want to continue to have the independence of living in their own home, but who want some extra security along with fewer of the responsibilities of independent living.

A sheltered-housing scheme has a warden living on the premises. The warden keeps an eye on the residents, reports any maintenance or repair problems, and organises the use of any communal facilities. Most schemes have an alarm system or intercom from each flat or bungalow to the warden's office, and the warden will summon outside help if necessary.

Sheltered housing is specifically designed to meet the needs of older people and will usually have such features as waist-height plug sockets, lifts as well as stairs, and handles on baths. The maintenance of the building and of the gardens is provided, and paid for with a service charge. There

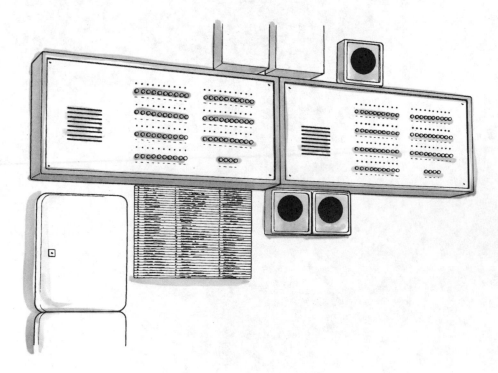

Alarm system connected to warden's office

will usually be communal facilities such as a laundry and a lounge. Schemes also provide a guest room for visitors.

A small amount of sheltered housing is available to rent from local authorities and from housing associations, but there is not enough to meet the demand. Local authorities and housing associations will assess people on the basis of need before deciding whether to offer housing. Private developers have responded to the growing need by building private sheltered-housing schemes, this housing being for sale. This section therefore concentrates on sheltered housing which is owner-occupied rather than that which is rented.

Owner-occupation

Some people, having sold a house which they have owned, are able to buy outright. For people who cannot buy outright, there are a number of options. Housing associations run **leasehold** schemes, where the older person buys a 70 per cent share of the lease. The other 30 per cent is funded with a subsidy from the government. When the flat or bungalow is sold again, the owner or the owner's estate receives 70 per cent of the value at that time. Some property developers offer discount schemes. Again, the owner will only receive a proportion of the price when the property is sold. It is important to have a solicitor or some other independent adviser check out this sort of scheme.

There is a code of practice called the Sheltered Housing Code which was introduced by the National House Building Council (NHBC) in April 1990. It is compulsory for all developers registered with the NHBC to comply with the code and therefore anyone buying a new property should

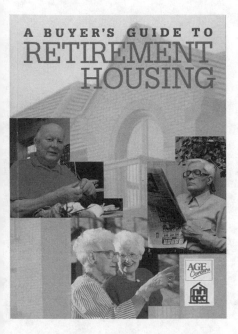

Age Concern provide information on retirement housing

Check the service charge on sheltered housing

make sure they buy from a builder who is registered. The basic requirements of the code are:

- the developer must provide a Purchaser's Information Pack. This will include details of
  - the names of the developer and the management organisation
  - the purchaser's legal rights
  - services and service charges and the 'sinking fund' (see below)
  - responsibilities of residents and the management organisation for repairs
  - the scheme manager's role and the alarm system
  - the consultation and complaints procedures
  - resale arrangements and charges;
- there must be a legally binding management agreement between the developer and the management organisation.

Sheltered housing involves a **service charge,** which is likely to go up each year with inflation. It can be paid monthly, quarterly or half-yearly. The amount will vary between schemes, depending on what is provided for the residents. It is quite likely, however, to be at least £20 a week. Typically this charge covers the wages of the warden, the insurance of the building, the heating of communal areas, maintenance costs, and the costs of administering the scheme. The Landlord and Tenant Act 1987 gives leaseholders the right to ask the County Court to set the cost of service charges where the residents feel the charges are too high or the services are inadequately provided.

Most sheltered-housing schemes have a fund for major and unexpected repairs, such as damage to the roof. This is known as a **sinking fund.** This may be financed by a contribution from the service charge, or the contribution may be made when the property is sold. In the latter case, a percentage of the sale value may be taken by the scheme.

The lease of a sheltered flat or bungalow will usually state that the property must be sold to someone over a certain age. The management committee may have to approve a buyer and may itself do the selling.

Sheltered-housing schemes do not offer help with personal care or domestic tasks. However, older people in sheltered housing can still make use of other services such as home helps, meals-on-wheels and community nursing services. Some schemes make a provision to move a resident out if he or she becomes very confused or in some way disruptive.

Sheltered housing with extra care

This is sometimes called **very sheltered housing** and is sometimes known as **extra-care sheltered housing.** Such schemes work on the same principles as sheltered housing, allowing people the freedom and independence of living in their own home, but also provide extra services such as meals and greater support. There is not yet very much of this type of provision. That which does exist tends to be provided by local authorities or housing associations.

These schemes do not provide nursing care. An older person needing this level of care may have to consider a move into a residential or nursing home.

> **TO DO**
> Find out about the sheltered-housing schemes available to older people in your area. It may be that most are for owner-occupation: try to find some which are available to rent.

TO FIND OUT

Write to some organisations offering sheltered housing. Ask for details.

Look carefully at the small print. Find out whether there are any rules, such as not allowing pets. What are the charges? Are there any extra charges? What happens to a resident who becomes confused? What are the rules about resale of properties?

The Elderly Accommodation Council produces directories of retirement housing for sale in different parts of the country. The organisation also provides information about retirement housing for rent and residential and nursing homes. The address and telephone number are included in the appendix to this book. A leaflet explaining the main aspects of the NHBC Sheltered Housing Code is available from the NHBC (address in appendix).

Finding out more: sheltered housing

★ Age Concern publishes an excellent booklet called *Housing Options for Older People*. This explains the different kinds of housing available, advises on ways money can be raised from a home, and discusses ways of getting repairs done.

★ Age Concern and the National Housing and Town Planning Council have produced a very useful booklet called *A Buyer's Guide to Retirement*. It gives information on all aspects of sheltered housing and includes details of other useful publications and addresses of organisations that can supply more information.

★ Age Concern also publishes a number of factsheets on aspects of retirement housing.

★ The Sheltered Housing Advisory and Conciliation Service (SHACS) is run in association with Age Concern England and offers specialist advice and information on retirement housing. The organisation will help solve management problems and act as a conciliation service in the case of difficulties between leaseholders and managers.

TO DO

Mrs Troyna is 67 years old. She has been recently widowed. She lives in a large Victorian house which was bought some thirty years ago. She is fit and quite active, but feels very nervous about being in the house alone. She is anxious about her future as she has no relatives close by. She asks your advice.

● Should she start to think about moving now, even though she is fit and active?
● What would be the best timescale for Mrs Troyna's plans?
● What sorts of factors should be looked at in choosing a new home?
● Which services need to be investigated or informed of any moves?
● How can any transitions be made as smooth as possible?

If you know someone in a similar sort of situation, think about this person instead.

A useful booklet for older people

Residential homes

There are three types of homes for older people: those run by the local authorities; those run by private organisations for profit; and those run by voluntary organisations. The number of places provided directly by local authorities is decreasing as national policy demands that local authorities use resources provided by the independent sector. In all cases the homes vary a great deal, in terms both of the type of accommodation and of the standard of care offered.

Residential homes have to be registered with the local authority and inspected twice a year. There are strict rules about the accommodation, the staffing levels and the standard of care provided. The owner of the home must prove that he or she is a fit person to run a home and that the facilities and staff are adequate for the number of residents catered for. If things are not as they should be, the **registration officer** can ask for changes to be made. Ultimately, the home can be closed down.

A code of practice was produced for the government by the Centre for Policy on Ageing. This gives guidelines on what rights older people should have in residential care. The booklet is called *Homelife*. It sets out a number of principles of care:

- the right to fulfilment;
- the right to dignity;
- the right to autonomy;
- the right to individuality;
- the right to esteem;
- the right to quality of experience;
- the right to take responsible risks.

There is also a companion code called *A Better Homelife* which covers residential and nursing homes. Both documents can be purchased from Bailey Distribution Ltd (address in appendix).

Local authority homes

It is quite difficult to get into a local authority elderly people's home. Pressure on places means that only those with the greatest need will be accepted.

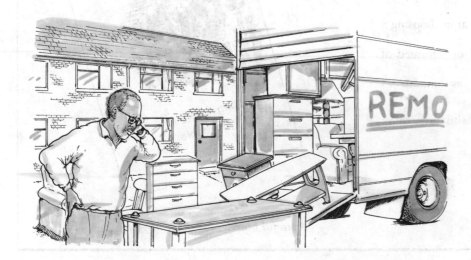

An older person might welcome advice on what to take into a residential home

TO DO

1 Arrange to visit three residential homes – one provided by social services, one run by a voluntary organisation and one which is privately owned. (Make contact with the homes, and arrange times when it would be convenient to make these visits.)

2 Compare the facilities and the care provided. Find out the admission criteria and the weekly cost in each case. Does this cost include everything?

TO FIND OUT

Are there any homes specifically designed to meet the needs of people from ethnic minorities? One source for this information is the Central Council for Jewish Social Service. Local Community Relations Councils may also be able to provide information.

Local authority homes are run by the social services departments and are sometimes known as **Part III accommodation**. This is because it was in Part III of the 1948 National Assistance Act that the government said that local authorities must provide accommodation for 'persons who by reason of age, infirmity, or any other circumstances are in need of care and attention which is not otherwise available to them'.

A home run by a local authority generally caters for at least twenty people; some are much larger. Some are purpose-built, others are converted from older buildings. There is usually an officer-in-charge, who is a trained social worker, and various other care staff. The aim is to create a home-like environment and to give people as much independence as possible.

Voluntary organisations

Voluntary organisations are those which are independent of the government and not working to make a profit. They vary a great deal, and sometimes provide services for a particular group of people – perhaps those who have worked in a particular occupation, or people of a particular religion. There are often waiting lists. Some of these homes provide nursing care, and some are part of larger complexes including sheltered housing.

Private homes

There has been a huge boom in private care of elderly people. Evidence of this can be seen in popular retirement areas such as Clacton, in Essex. The increase in provision is partly a result of the increased number of elderly people. An important boost to the private sector came in 1983 when the government changed the rules about benefits, allowing money to be paid for people to stay in private homes.

Paying for care

Under the 1990 NHS and Community Care Act (implemented in 1993), people who can afford to pay for residential care are expected to do so. An assessment will be carried out to decide how much is to be paid. The assessment is based on income and savings and other assets such as a house.

People with a low income are entitled to income support (see Chapter 4). For people in private or voluntary homes there is an additional residential allowance to help pay the costs.

If the person's weekly income is more than the cost of the home, then he or she will have to pay the full amount. If the income is less and the person has savings or assets below £10 000, the local authority should make up the difference in the amount. A small personal expenses allowance is allowed in the calculation, so that the person will have a weekly sum to pay for clothing, toiletries and small luxuries. The personal expenses allowance was £13.75 per week in 1996.

People can keep £10 000 of savings or assets before starting to contribute to the cost of care. Those with savings between £10 000 and £16 000 pay a contribution. Savings over £16 000 mean that people pay the full cost of their care.

When someone moves permanently into residential care, their home counts as part of their assets and therefore will usually be sold to pay for the care. This does not apply if a husband, wife or other elderly or disabled relative is living in the house.

Social services will have a list of approved homes for which they will pay their share of the costs. If someone wants to go into a more expensive home, relatives can top up the fees to make this possible.

Finding out more: residential homes

★ Counsel and Care for the Elderly is an organisation which can provide advice and information for people thinking about moving into a residential or nursing home. Counsel and Care has lists of private and voluntary homes which are suitable for people in different circumstances and with particular needs. Counsel and Care produces factsheets on aspects of residential care.

★ Age Concern publishes an excellent booklet called *Finding and Paying for Residential and Nursing Home Care*, as well as various factsheets on care for older people.

WORDCHECK

sheltered housing A housing scheme which provides extra services, such as a warden.

service charge A payment made by occupants of sheltered housing to cover costs of services such as the warden and routine maintenance.

sinking fund A fund to cover major and unexpected expenses of sheltered housing, such as roof repairs.

Part III accommodation A term sometimes used to describe local authority provision for older people.

registration officer The person responsible for registering private- and voluntary-sector homes for older people and others.

TO DO

Consider the situation of a client who is an older person living in the community. (This can be a real person you work with or an imagined person, in which case you should describe the situation – housing, support and the like – and the personality, likes and dislikes of the person.) Imagine that the client is about to move into a residential home. How would you support him or her in this move?

- In visiting prospective homes, what would you look for? Compile a checklist of points which might indicate the quality of care offered.
- How could you help him or her to make the best use of a visit?
- Would a trial stay be helpful?
- What preparations would need to be made?
- How could links with the community be maintained?

TO FIND OUT

Contact the county council and find out about current plans for residential services for older people.

3 Health

The term **health care** tends to make people think of hospitals and surgeries, doctors and nurses. Yet most health care is provided not by professionals, but by relatives and friends. Relatives and friends are usually the first to be consulted when someone feels unwell; the doctors come second. A lot of basic nursing is not in fact done by nurses, but by untrained women in their roles as mothers, partners and daughters.

For some people, there may be no relatives or friends to turn to. This may be the case for an older person who is alone and isolated; or for someone who has spent some time in a hospital – perhaps a hospital for people with mental illnesses or learning disabilities; or for a young person who has come out of care, or who has had to leave his or her family. In these situations it may be the care worker who is asked for help. An elderly person may tell you that she needs dental care but does not feel able to get to the surgery. An adult with learning difficulties may not be happy with his doctor, and you may be the first to know about it. You may suspect that someone is worrying about her use of drugs or fears he has AIDS. In these situations it would be useful to know where to find information and whom to turn to.

This chapter provides information on various aspects of health care. The focus is on the various services which are available. Much of the health care we need is provided by the **National Health Service (NHS)**. Consequently there are sections describing the organisation of the health service and the various services within it. The NHS is dominated by one type of medicine, sometimes known as **Western medicine** or **orthodox medicine**. Some people choose **alternative treatments** and there is a section describing these, with suggested methods of finding further information. There is also a section describing ways of obtaining orthodox medical treatment outside the NHS.

As with everything else, health issues change. Diseases disappear, because of vaccinations or drugs or with changes in living standards. New health problems emerge. The most shocking and terrible in recent times was the discovery of the fatal effects of AIDS. Faced with a new problem, large government organisations are slow to respond. It is often voluntary organisations which lead the field in meeting new needs. The Terrence Higgins Trust is one such example. This organisation was established after the death of Terrence Higgins, who died of AIDS in 1982. At that time there was very little information and support available. The Trust was set up by his friends to fill this gap. It has since grown very rapidly, and now meets many of the non-medical needs of people with HIV and AIDS, particularly in Greater London.

In most areas of health there are voluntary organisations working. Often a given organisation is concerned specifically with one illness and provides special expertise in this area. Some organisations are self-help

Local voluntary groups help people with health problems. Cancerlink can provide information on starting a group to support people with cancer

groups which allow people to talk with others who share the same problems and worries. This is especially important with illnesses which carry some kind of stigma, as do AIDS and mental illnesses.

The special needs of particular groups of people are increasingly being recognised. There are **Well Woman clinics** in many areas to provide preventive health care for women. In some areas there are **link services** within the NHS for people from ethnic minorities. A link worker will be based in a clinic or health centre and will aim to help overcome the language and cultural barriers between patients and doctors and nurses. Such workers are usually employed by health authorities in areas where a lot of Asian people live. There are also sources of information on particular diseases, such as sickle-cell anaemia which is more commonly found amongst people of African origin.

Finding out more: health-care provision

★   There is a vast number of voluntary organisations concerned with health. The following directories provide information on groups with addresses:

- The *Charities Digest* is published annually by Waterlow Information Services.
- The Patients Association publishes *The Health Address Book* which is a directory of self-help and support organisations.
- *Voluntary Agencies* is published by the National Council for Voluntary Organisations.

Most of these books are updated annually and are available in libraries. Health promotion departments would also have information on voluntary groups.

★   *Your Health, A Guide to Services for Women* is a free publication from the Department of Health. It can be obtained by writing to the Department of Health or phoning the leaflets line (see appendix).

★   Further information on issues related to black and Asian people can be obtained from the Commission for Racial Equality.

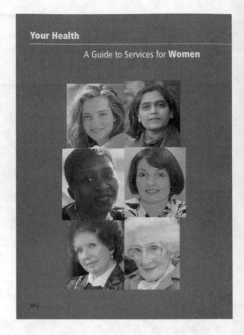

Particular emphasis has been placed on women's health

3.1 Advice and information on health care

For many people the first source of advice and information on health care is not an expert or a professional, nor a service set up to give specialist advice. People tend to turn first to those around them – relatives or friends. 'Do you think I should see a doctor?' 'Which dentist do you go to?' 'Do you know of a practice with a woman doctor?' 'How did you find a psychotherapist?' But some people do not have friends or relatives they can turn to. Some problems are too difficult, and need more specialised information. Sometimes people do not want to worry or frighten the people they love. Some illnesses – such as AIDS and mental illnesses – carry a stigma and people dare not ask for help from the people they know. This section describes the various sources of advice and information.

Some areas have **health information services**. These may be based in libraries, hospitals or health centres. They contain collections of books, articles and leaflets on all aspects of health. All health authorities have **health promotion departments**. (These used to be known as 'health education departments'.) In some areas they tend to focus on providing information for health-care workers, but some provide more of a public service. They keep literature on health education (smoking, diet, exercise and the like) and information on local groups concerned with health issues. Each **Health Authority** has a **Community Health Council (CHC)**. This is made up of twelve members, whose job is to represent the local community in the health service. As well as being consulted in decision-making, they deal with complaints and provide information on local health services.

The media are also a source of information on health issues. Two examples are the BBC Radio 4 programmes *Does He Take Sugar?*, for people with disabilities, and *In Touch*, for people with a visual handicap. There are also frequent television documentaries on health problems and

BACUP provides information for people with cancer

issues. Problem pages in newspapers and magazines are another popular source of information, especially on issues where people are afraid to ask anyone they know, including sometimes even their doctor.

Telephone **helplines** are becoming more common. There are commercial lines which provide taped information, but these are quite expensive – costing more than an ordinary long-distance call. There are also helplines which are free, for example the National Aids Helpline. Here the service offers information and advice for people worried about AIDS. It is not a pre-recorded service, but deals with individual enquiries. There are also local **Aidslines** in most areas. Many voluntary organisations specialising in particular conditions offer telephone helplines. One example is the Motor Neurone Disease Phoneline. There is also DIAL – Disablement Information and Advice Lines – which is run *by* people with disabilities *for* people with disabilities. There are over fifty groups throughout the country.

For most serious illnesses and conditions there is a voluntary organisation specialising in that area. Because these are so specialised, they are likely to know far more about the illness and the resources available to help than any general practitioner (GP) or general nurse could know. They can also provide the special understanding of people who have been in the same position. Often they offer to put people in touch with each other, to share ideas and to provide mutual support. For example, there are two organisations which specialise in providing information on cancer. One is BACUP (the British Association of Cancer United Patients). The second is Cancerlink. Each provides a newsletter and information booklets with practical advice and information. BACUP has a telephone helpline staffed by nurses. Cancerlink supports local self-help groups with training and assistance.

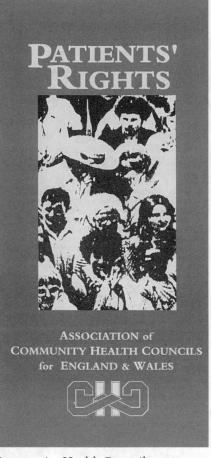

PATIENTS' RIGHTS

ASSOCIATION of
COMMUNITY HEALTH COUNCILS
for ENGLAND & WALES

*Community Health Councils represent
the local community in the health service*

WORDCHECK

Western or **orthodox medicine** The type of medicine practised in the NHS, which tends to emphasise the treatment of symptoms with drugs.

alternative or **complementary medicine** Forms of treatment other than Western or orthodox medicine.

stigma Something which sets a person apart and causes feelings of embarrassment or shame.

voluntary organisation An organisation which has not been set up by a government body and which does not aim to make a profit.

Well Woman clinics Clinics that provide preventive health checks for women.

link services Services provided by some health authorities to help people from ethnic minorities use the health service.

health information services Information services provided for the public by some health authorities, based perhaps in a hospital or health centre.

health promotion departments Services that provide information and health education.

Community Health Councils (CHCs) Groups who represent the local community on health matters within the NHS.

helplines Telephone advice services.

TO DO

1 Design a questionnaire to find out where people get information on health and health care.

● List as many sources as you can think of. Which of these have they used in the last six months? Include a category for 'Any other'.

● You might also like to find out whether people were happy with the information sources they used, and whether they would like more information to be offered.

2 Ask as many and as varied people as possible to complete your questionnaire.

3 If your results prove interesting you could send them to the local Community Health Council.

The Medical Advisory Service publishes pamphlets on various health issues

Finding out more: health care

★ The Patients' Association gives advice to patients and publishes leaflets on health issues.
★ The Medical Advisory Service provides advice and information to the public on any medical or healthcare matter. It also runs helplines and publishes a newsletter and leaflets on various health issues.

3.2 The organisation of the NHS

The NHS is a massive organisation. It is the largest employer in the UK. Not surprisingly, it has a complicated structure of management. This section describes the national structure of the health service.

Although most people use the health service reasonably successfully without understanding the overall structure, an overview can help in finding your way around the maze of different services and professionals. It can help also in understanding the major changes which have taken place in the health service.

These changes were a result of the 1990 NHS and Community Care Act. The key aspects of the Act were the creation of independent **NHS Trusts** – hospitals and other units which opt out of the control of the Health Authority – and the possibility for doctors in general practice to become **fund-holders**, spending their funds on hospital and other services.

At the national level

The person ultimately responsible for the health service in Parliament is the Secretary of State for Health. He or she is the head of the **Department of Health Policy Board**, which is responsible for running the NHS in England. In Scotland, Wales and Northern Ireland there are separate Secretaries of State.

The Policy Board divides the money available for the NHS between the various regions of the country. There is also a board of directors of the NHS called the **NHS Management Committee**. This is in charge of the day-to-day running of the service.

At the regional level

England has eight **Regional Offices** which plan and monitor services for their region. They give money to **Health Authorities** and the GPs who manage their own funds. The new trusts – hospitals or other services which have opted out of Health Authority control – are responsible directly to the NHS Management Committee.

At the district level

Under the Regional Office there are Health Authorities which purchase services at a local level, mainly from local NHS Trusts, but also from private providers. The Health Authorities also monitor the quality of services provided by the Trusts and oversee services provided by GPs, NHS dentists, chemists and opticians.

Trusts

Most hospitals are now run as **NHS Trusts**. Trusts are managed independently and compete to win contracts to treat patients, who are paid for by Health Authorities or by fund-holding GPs.

Other community services, such as clinics and community psychiatric services, are also organised into NHS Trusts.

TO DO

Find out the local structure of the NHS.

- Where is the local Regional Office?
- Which is the local Health Authority?
- How are services managed by the Health Authority? They may be split into units covering different areas of health care.
- Which areas of health care do the local Trusts cover?
- Which doctors hold their own budgets?

This information should be available from the Health Authority and from the Community Health Council. Addresses and phone numbers can be found in the *Yellow Pages* under 'Health authorities and

Doctors

Similarly, there are now two types of GP. **Fund-holding GPs** are financed directly from the Regional Office. They can send patients to any hospital which seems to offer the best-value service. The bill is paid by the GP. **Non-fund-holding GPs** are funded by the Health Authority. They can send patients to hospitals with which the Health Authority has a contract. If the treatment needed is not available at this hospital, patients can be sent elsewhere, so long as the Health Authority is prepared to pay.

WORDCHECK

NHS trusts Hospitals or groups of services which have opted out of the control of the Health Authority.

Department of Health Policy Board The national decision-making body for the NHS.

Secretary of State for Health The government minister responsible for the NHS.

NHS Management Committee The board of directors concerned with the day-to-day running of the NHS at a national level.

fund-holding GPs General practitioners who have opted to control funds for their practice. These are used to buy services from hospitals and elsewhere.

Finding out more: the NHS

★ *The Patient's Charter and You* is a free booklet which sets out patients' entitlements to various aspects of health care. The address to write to is included in the appendix under 'The Patient's Charter and You'.

★ The Institute of Health Services Management publishes the *Hospitals and Health Services Year Book* annually. It should be available in college libraries.

The Patient's Charter sets out rights to health care

3.3 The services provided by the NHS

There are many different professionals working in the health service providing a wide range of services. This section describes the main services. Within the NHS, these include:

- GPs;
- dentists;
- chemists;
- opticians;
- district nurses;
- health visitors;
- community psychiatric nurses;
- midwives;
- chiropodists and podiatrists;
- Well Woman clinics;
- hospitals;
- occupational therapists;
- physiotherapists;
- speech therapists.

There are also psychologists, psychiatrists and psychotherapists. (Services for people with mental illness are covered in a separate section.) Social workers are also based in hospitals and mental health centres.

General practitioners (GPs)

GPs are independent and self-employed, but contracted to the health service. They are paid on the basis of the number of patients they have. Everyone has the right to register with a GP, and most of the services provided are free.

GPs are important as a means of access to other parts of the health service. They diagnose and treat everyday illnesses and conditions, but they also refer people to hospitals and other forms of more specialised care. Although some rural GPs still work alone, most are in group practices or health centres. A health centre will have a team of medical workers – usually including nurses, health visitors and midwives – as well as doctors. Increasingly, the teams are coming to include counsellors and social workers as well.

Everyone has the right to change their GP for any reason. Lists of local GPs are kept by the Health Authority: these give details of the sex, qualifications and year of qualifying of each doctor. Details of the surgery hours are also listed. These lists are available from the Health Authority or in libraries and Citizens' Advice Bureaux. Additional patients' rights are set out in The Patient's Charter (see below) and many doctors now have their own charters which help patients make use of the services offered.

Finding out more: patients' rights

★ There is a leaflet called *Patients' Rights*. It is published by the Association of Community Health Councils, and is available in Welsh, Hindi, Punjabi, Gujarati, Urdu, Cantonese, Turkish, Vietnamese and Greek as well as English.

★ *The Patient's Charter and You* sets out patients' entitlements to health care. People who think their charter rights are being denied can write to Alan Langlands, Chief Executive of the NHS at the Patient's Charter Unit (address in the appendix).

Dentists

Not all dentists provide NHS treatment and it is necessary to check this before registering with a dentist. Dentists providing treatment under the NHS are available in most areas, although some are not able to take on new NHS patients. It may be necessary to try more than one dentist before finding one who will provide NHS treatment. The local Health Authority can help people who are not registered with a dentist to find one. The Health Authority can also provide other information such as which dentists have facilities which are accessible to people in wheelchairs.

Patients register with a dentist in a similar way to registering with a doctor. This involves signing on for *continuing care and treatment* for a period of two years. There is no cost involved in signing on. Dentists are paid for each continuing-care patient they have on their lists. Continuing-care patients are entitled to the full range of treatment available. They are entitled to free replacement or repair of most dental work if something goes wrong within a year. It is also possible to sign on as an *occasional patient*, for example if you need a dentist whilst on holiday. In this case you are not entitled to receive the full range of treatment.

Dentists must provide an information leaflet. This will explain how the practice works, including facilities for home visits and emergency treatment. People who are registered are entitled to home visits if this is necessary.

The Community Dental Service provides a safety net for people who do not find it easy to visit a dentist, perhaps for reasons of disability. A dentist may refer a patient to the Community Dental Service. The CDS works in residential homes as well as visiting people at home. For more information about the CDS locally, look in the *Yellow Pages* under 'NHS' for the Community Dental Service Manager or phone the free NHS helpline on 0800 665544.

If specialist hospital treatment is needed, a referral is made by the dentist or the Community Dental Service.

Dental treatment is not usually free. People have to pay for 80 per cent of the cost of all treatment, including examinations and X-rays. There is however a limit to the amount which can be paid for one course of treatment, and some groups of people are **exempt** from payment. These are:

- all young people under 18;
- young people under 19 in full-time education;
- pregnant women;
- women with a baby under one year old;
- people on certain means-tested benefits.

These people automatically get free treatment. Others on a low income can claim help with the costs.

Dentists must provide a treatment plan with details of costs. The patient does not have to decide immediately whether to go ahead, but can take this home for further thought.

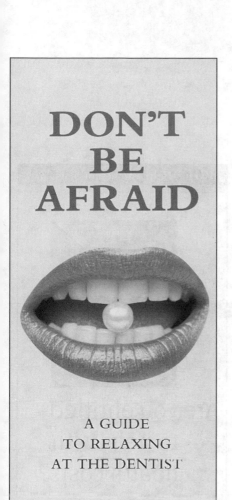

DON'T BE AFRAID

A GUIDE
TO RELAXING
AT THE DENTIST

The British Dental Health Foundation aims to improve public awareness of dental health

Finding out more: dental care

★   For more information on help with dental costs, see the leaflet published by the Department of Health. It is available from social security offices, doctors and dentists, and by writing to the Department of Health.

★   Age Concern produces information leaflets on dental care for elderly people.

★   The British Dental Health Foundation (address in appendix) produces leaflets on all aspects of dental care which help patients understand their treatment and care for their teeth.

Chemists

Some drugs can be bought over the counter from any chemist. For others a prescription from a doctor is needed. As with dental treatments, prescriptions are not free. The charge is made per item. But again certain categories of people receive free prescriptions. These are:

- children under 16;
- students under 19 in full-time education;
- people on certain means-tested benefits;
- people over 60;
- people on a war pension;
- pregnant women;
- women with a baby under 12 months of age;
- people on a low income.

People with certain long-lasting illnesses or conditions also receive free medication. These include diabetes and epilepsy.

People who do not qualify for exemption from payment but who need a lot of drugs can get a kind of **season ticket** for their prescriptions. These can be bought either for a four-month period or for one year. They are worth having if you are likely to need more than five items in four months, or more than fourteen items in one year.

Finding out more: prescription costs

★   The Department of Health produces leaflets on entitlement to free prescriptions. The leaflets are available in social security offices, doctors surgeries or can be obtained by phoning the leaflets line on 0800 555777 or writing to the Department of Health (the address is included in the appendix).

Opticians

Like dentists, opticians contract with the Health Authority to provide services under the National Health Service. They test eyesight, write prescriptions for glasses, and sell glasses. Eye tests are free only to the following categories of people:

- children under 16;
- students under 19 in full-time education;
- people on certain means-tested benefits;
- people who are registered blind or partially sighted;
- people over 40 who have a parent, brother or sister with glaucoma.

HC11   Help with health costs

Are you entitled to help with health costs?

- NHS prescriptions
- NHS dental treatment
- sight tests, glasses and contact lenses
- travel to hospital for NHS treatment
- NHS wigs and fabric supports

NHS

The Department of Health publishes leaflets on help with health costs

---

TO DO

Make a survey of the local opticians, looking for the best bargains. How much do they charge for a sight test? Compare the prices of spectacles at the opticians with those in other shops.

There is no set fee for an eye test, but it is likely to cost around £17 (1996). If glasses are needed, the optician will make out a prescription. This can be used to get glasses from that optician or any other.

People who are eligible for a free sight test and who are housebound can have a home visit by the optician free of charge. Others can get help with the cost of a home visit.

NHS vouchers are available to help with the cost of the test and the glasses. People who automatically get a voucher are:

- people under 16;
- people between 16 and 19 and in full-time education;
- people on certain means-tested benefits.

Others can claim help if on a low income. The vouchers are for varying amounts. They may be used in part-payment for glasses if someone wants to buy a more expensive pair. In some circumstances, people can qualify for contact lenses rather than glasses.

Finding out more: eye care

★ The Department of Health produces a leaflet on help with sight tests and glasses. The leaflet is available in social security offices, doctors or opticians or can be obtained by phoning the leaflets line on 0800 555777 or writing to the Department of Health (the address is included in the appendix).

District nurses

District nurses provide nursing care for people in their own homes. Their patients may be people who have been recently discharged from hospital, or people with disabilities who need nursing care and who would perhaps find it difficult to get to a health centre. Although district nurses may be attached to health centres they are employed by the Health Authority, not by the doctors. Often it is a doctor who arranges for a district nurse to visit a patient.

Health visitors

Health visitors are trained nurses, but the focus of their work is not on practical nursing. Rather they are concerned with health education. They mostly work with mothers of babies and young children, monitoring welfare and providing advice and support. Some health visitors work with older people or people with disabilities.

Community psychiatric nurses

These nurses provide support and counselling for people with mental illnesses who are living in the community. They also administer drugs. They may work through doctors or through a central mental-health centre. They see patients in the patients' own homes or at a centre. Some work with groups as well as individuals.

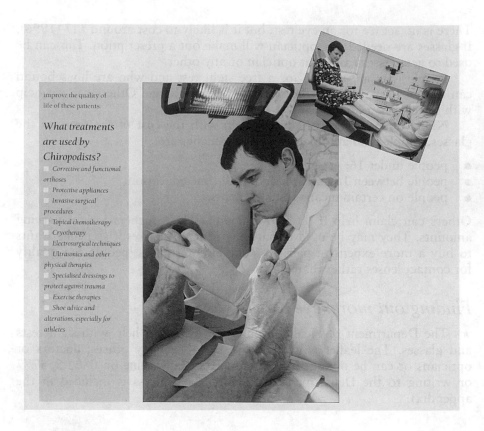

What treatments
are used by
Chiropodists?

☐ Corrective and functional
orthoses
☐ Protective appliances
☐ Invasive surgical
procedures
☐ Topical chemotherapy
☐ Cryotherapy
☐ Electrosurgical techniques
☐ Ultrasonics and other
physical therapies
☐ Specialised dressings to
protect against trauma
☐ Exercise therapies
☐ Shoe advice and
alterations, especially for
athletes

Chiropodists help people care for their feet

Midwives

Midwives are often based in hospitals but some work in the community. They help pregnant women with antenatal care, deliver babies, and are involved in postnatal care when the baby has been born.

Chiropodists and podiatrists

Chiropodists work on problems people may have with their feet. (The more up-to-date term for chiropodist is podiatrist.) Most people have to pay to see a chiropodist privately, but the following people are entitled to free treatment:

- people over 60;
- schoolchildren;
- pregnant women;
- people with disabilities.

People may be referred by a doctor or they may contact a chiropodist themselves. There is often a waiting list for treatment. Chiropodists may visit older people in residential homes or at day centres.

Occupational therapists (OTs)

Some occupational therapists work within social services departments. Others are based in the health service, often working from hospitals. OTs are involved with the assessment of disability. They advise people with disabilities on how best to cope with the activities of daily living. Home loan equipment can be recommended to make practical activities easier (for more on this see Chapter 5). Some areas have a centre, perhaps in a

TO DO

1 Find out what sort of hospitals there are in the local community.

- There will be a district general hospital. What facilities does it have?
- Is there a psychiatric hospital locally?
- Is there a day hospital? If you work with people who attend a day hospital, it might be possible to arrange a visit for yourself.
- Is there a local cottage hospital?

2 Consider these hospitals from your clients' points of view.

- How would they feel about entering these hospitals?
- How would you reassure them?
- Is there anything you could do to make a hospital visit easier?

TO DO

With the help of your supervisor, identify five clients of varying ages and circumstances.

- Consider each client's involvement with the health services.
- List the staff with whom the client is involved.
- What is the role of each of the health workers?
- Are there any gaps? Any unmet needs? Any areas of unnecessary overlap?
- Is the client happy with the service he or she is getting?
- Is there any way in which the client could get a better deal from the health service?

hospital, where people can see and experiment with the various aids and adaptations which are available. These can be bought or sometimes borrowed. OTs also run groups for people in hospitals and in the community. These might cover such areas as cookery or anxiety management.

Physiotherapists

Physiotherapists usually work from hospitals. They help people in their recovery from injuries, recommending and teaching exercises to help muscles and joints.

Hospitals

Hospitals vary in size and in the facilities and services they provide. Each district has a **district general hospital**. This will usually have a maternity ward, an out-patient clinic, X-ray and other facilities, occupational therapists and speech therapists. Such hospitals tend to treat **acute** patients – that is, those needing short-term treatment. Some district general hospitals also have wards for people with psychiatric illnesses.

Other types of hospital may be available in the area. **Cottage hospitals** are small hospitals with less emphasis on technical treatment for diagnosis and surgery. They may provide day surgery or be used for rehabilitation after a stay in a general hospital. There are also **day hospitals**, used for minor operations. Some areas have day hospitals for people with a mental illness.

Many towns have a large **psychiatric hospital**. In the past these hospitals provided long-term care for large numbers of people. Most also had acute wards. Over the last few years the numbers of people living in these hospitals have been reduced as patients have been moved out into the local community. Most such hospitals are scheduled for closure. The same applies to so-called 'mental-handicap hospitals' for people with learning difficulties. Increasingly people with learning difficulties are cared for in smaller units in the community.

WORDCHECK

district nurse Someone who provides nursing care in people's own homes.
health visitor Someone who provides health education, usually for families with small children or elderly people.
community psychiatric nurse Someone who provides support and nursing for people with mental-health problems who are living in the community.
occupational therapist Someone who helps people with disabilities to live a normal life, teaching necessary skills and providing special equipment.
physiotherapist Someone who helps people with injuries, teaching them appropriate exercises.

3.4 Sex and health care

Contraception

Health Authorities are responsible for provision of advice on contraception and supplying forms of contraception. All contraceptive advice, medical check-ups and treatments are free.

Family doctors provide contraceptive services free to women although they do not usually provide condoms.

The Family Planning Association provides information on sex education, relationships and on contraception. Their services are available to the public or to professionals in health care through local clinics. Brook Advisory Centres specialise in providing advice on birth control and counselling on emotional problems with relationships for young people under 25. The voluntary organisations listed below provide help with contraceptives as well as an abortion service.

If a woman thinks she is at risk of an unplanned pregnancy, emergency contraception can be given within three or five days (depending on the method used) after sex has taken place. This can only be provided by a doctor – either the GP or possibly at the accident and emergency unit of a hospital.

Abortion

Abortions can be arranged on the National Health Service through a GP. Alternatively there are voluntary organisations working in this area.

The British Pregnancy Advisory Service (BPAS) helps women who are legally eligible for an abortion and who wish to be treated privately or those whose doctor will not arrange an abortion under the NHS. There are branches throughout the country and a national helpline.

The Pregnancy Advisory Service has an abortion clinic and offers free counselling to women having abortions.

Marie Stopes International offers abortion services in London, Leeds and Manchester as well as free pregnancy testing and emergency contraceptives.

Sexually transmitted diseases (STDs)

Local genito-urinary medicine (GUM) clinics are attached to hospitals and all treatment is free and completely confidential. Clinics are listed in *The Phone Book* under GUM, STD or special clinics. A list of clinics can be obtained from the local Health Authority, a GP or by writing to the Health Education Authority. As well as sexually transmitted diseases, the clinics deal with other kinds of genital and urinary conditions. (See also section 3.7 on HIV and AIDS.)

Finding out more

★ Leaflets on contraception, sexually transmitted diseases and safer sex are produced by the Family Planning Association.

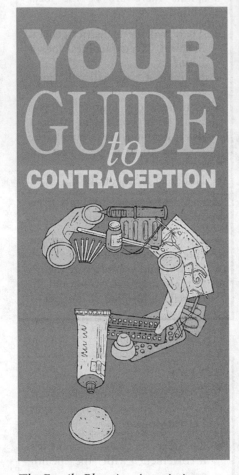

The Family Planning Association provides information on contraception

3.5 Special services for people who are terminally ill

People with terminal illnesses are likely to be using many of the NHS services described earlier in this chapter. However there are also specialised organisations which have been set up to meet the special needs of people with terminal illnesses.

Hospices

There are more than a hundred hospices in Britain. They provide care for people with terminal illnesses – often, but not always, people with cancer. They are often run by voluntary organisations and depend on donations from the public. There are also, however, hospices within the NHS.

Hospices aim to provide a style of care very different from that found in a hospital. Hospitals tend to be very busy places, full of hustle and bustle. They are orientated to curing patients. They are increasingly reliant on technology and are full of technical equipment for diagnosis and treatment. In contrast, hospices provide a calm and restful atmosphere. They are usually in attractive buildings with tranquil gardens and grounds. Nurses are never too busy to stop and listen. The aim is not to try to cure illnesses but to help patients to be as comfortable as possible. Hospices are very informal, with few rules and everything geared as far as possible to the needs of the individual patients.

Hospices have developed a system of preventive pain control. The philosophy is that there is no need for a patient to experience pain. Where hospital staff might administer drugs once pain is felt, the hospice method is to give the drugs before the pain starts. This is done by working out an individual programme of pain relief to help each patient. The same applies to other unpleasant symptoms of illness.

Hospice staff are involved in training other health-care professionals in their approach. Many hospices are also developing home-care facilities and day centres so that people can benefit from hospice methods whilst remaining at home.

TO DO

1 Find out whether there is a hospice near you. The Hospice Information Service has details of all the hospices. The *1997 Directory of Hospice and Palliative Care Services* includes details of all the services available for people with terminal illnesses, at home and in hospices. A large stamped addressed envelope must be sent for a copy of the directory.

2 It may be possible to visit a local hospice. Some hold regular seminars at which they explain their methods of care. They are interested in helping others, such as workers in homes for older people, to develop the philosophy of care and the skills used in the hospice movement.

3.6 Special services for people with cancer

Nursing Care

Macmillan nurses work with people with cancer and with their relatives in the community. Initially each nurse is funded by a voluntary organisation called Cancer Relief, but it is expected that after three years the health service will take over the financing. There are over five hundred Macmillan nurses working in Britain. A few are based in hospitals but most work alongside GPs and other nurses in the community. They are specially trained, and provide emotional support as well as nursing care. Like the hospices, they specialise in pain and symptom control.

Cancer Relief also provides 14 cancer-care units with in-patient wards, day-care centres and out-patient facilities.

Marie Curie Cancer Care also provide nursing care by day and night in patients' homes. There are around 5000 Marie Curie nurses working throughout the country. Patients are referred to the organisation by district nurses. Marie Curie Cancer Care also runs 11 hospices around the country.

Support

BACUP is an organisation that helps people with cancer and helps their families and friends to live with cancer. BACUP provides support by telephone and letter, information and advice and a counselling service. All the services are free to people with cancer as well as their families and friends.

Cancerlink is a resource for some 500 support and self-help groups throughout the country and provides publications on cancer and advice and support over the telephone.

The Cancer Care Society has a national network of social and emotional support groups for people with cancer and their families. Trained counsellors provide telephone and personal counselling. The society will also put people in touch with each other through the telephone.

Cruse offers counselling, social contact, support and advice to anyone who has experienced the death of someone they care about. Cruse has local branches in most areas of the country and a national newsletter.

A holistic approach to cancer

Information on the Bristol Cancer Help Centre is included in section 3.12.

Finding out more: services for people with cancer

★ For information on Macmillan nurses, contact Cancer Relief Macmillan Fund. The fund also produces a leaflet on other sources of help and support.

★ BACUP produces booklets on all aspects of cancer. Write for a list of their publications.

Macmillan nurses care for people at all stages of their illness, not just those with terminal cancer

A number of voluntary organisations provide support, advice and care for people with cancer and their relatives

3.7 Special services for people with HIV and AIDS

All the services which have been looked at in previous sections are available to people with **Human Immuno-deficiency Virus** (**HIV**) and those with **Acquired Immune Deficiency Syndrome** (**AIDS**). There are also, however, some services which have been set up specially to help people with HIV and AIDS. Some of the specialist services, including health promotion, advice and information, are provided by NHS Trusts; others are offered by voluntary organisations. One positive outcome from AIDS is that it has encouraged a new kind of service delivery, in which people are very involved in the decision-making about their care and treatment.

Advice and information

There is a national **AIDS helpline** which keeps up-to-date information on all aspects of HIV and AIDS. Phone calls are free and the service can be used at any time. At certain times advice is given in Arabic and Asian languages. In most areas there is also a local **Aidsline**. The phone number may be found in *The Phone Book*.

Health Authorities have AIDS and HIV co-ordinators. These people are often based in health promotion departments. They can provide advice and information on local and national services. Health promotion departments provide leaflets and keep libraries from which books on all aspects of health can be borrowed. The main specialist organisation working in the area of HIV and AIDS is the *Terrence Higgins Trust*. This has grown very rapidly and now provides a wide range of services. One of the services is a telephone helpline staffed by trained counsellors who can offer advice, information and help. The Terrence Higgins Trust has a large library of books, videos, press cuttings, journals and newsletters, and information stored on computer databases. Anyone can make an appointment to use the library.

Another voluntary organisation in the field is *Positively Women* which offers support, counselling and information to women with HIV or AIDS. Positively Women has a helpline which operates from 12.00 to 14.00 Mondays to Fridays (the number is included in the appendix). There are also organisations to meet the needs of black people with HIV and AIDS, for example *Blackliners* and *Black HIV and AIDS Network*.

Finding out more: HIV and AIDS

★   For free literature about HIV and AIDS there is a freephone service, tel. 0800 555777. The postal address is PO Box 5000, Glasgow G12 90DL.
★   The Terrence Higgins Trust publishes a number of leaflets on aspects of HIV and AIDS. Write for a list of publications.

Support

The Terrence Higgins Trust provides a number of different forms of support. One is the **buddy scheme**, which was first developed in the USA. Buddies work voluntarily and have training and support groups. They provide practical help and emotional support. Their aim is to help the person with AIDS to achieve the best possible quality of life and to remain as independent as possible. Whilst the Terrence Higgins Trust operates in Greater London, other organisations in most parts of the country have set up buddy schemes working in a similar way.

Most of the organisations involved with HIV and AIDS have set up support groups. These exist for people with HIV and AIDS and also for their families and partners. The Terrence Higgins Trust also offers a counselling service. Some Health Authorities have set up **home-care teams** to help people with AIDS remain at home. The telephone helplines will be able to give information on the local availability of services.

Day centres in London

London has several day centres for people with AIDS. One is the London Lighthouse which offers a meeting place for people with AIDS. Partners, friends and families are also welcome. There are lounges and gardens. Services are available such as counselling and workshops on various issues. The London Lighthouse is open seven days a week.

Residential care

Hospices have been set up specifically for people with AIDS. One is the residential unit at the London Lighthouse. People can stay for short or long periods. It provides a pleasant and comfortable environment without the institutional features of a hospital. Anyone can apply for a place; admission will be considered on the basis of need.

The Mildmay Mission Hospital is a Christian charitable organisation but it cares for anyone in need. It has a homely atmosphere with single rooms and communal facilities. As with the London Lighthouse, people are accepted on the basis of need and urgency.

Finding out more: working with HIV and AIDS

★ There is a manual on all aspects of HIV and AIDS, prepared for organisations working in this area. It is updated regularly. There is a reduced price for voluntary organisations and the manual can be used in the libraries referred to above. It is called the *National AIDS Manual*, and is available from NAM Publications Ltd.

The Terrence Higgins Trust provides information on all aspects of HIV and AIDS

TO THINK ABOUT

1 What support and guidance would you offer to someone who thought he or she might be HIV-positive?

2 Do you have any fears or prejudices which might make this difficult for you?

3 How could relatives or close friends be best supported?

WORDCHECK

hospices Residential centres which provide care for people who are dying.

Macmillan nurses A group of nurses who specialise in caring for people with cancer.

helplines Telephone advice services.

health promotion departments Services providing information and health education.

NHS trusts Hospitals or groups of services which have opted out of the control of the health authority.

buddy scheme A scheme that provides support for people with AIDS.

3.8 Special services for people with alcohol-related problems

Most people drink alcohol. Apart from the odd hangover, drinking is pleasurable and in most cases seems to do little damage. However, a minority of people drink excessively or inappropriately, and it is these people who are described as having **alcohol-related problems**. Alcohol is a poison which, in excess, causes damage to the liver and to other parts of the body, including the brain. The government has produced guidelines for sensible drinking – these suggest a weekly limit to the number of *units of alcohol* for men and women. (One unit is equivalent to half a pint of ordinary strength beer, lager or cider, a small glass of wine, a single measure of spirits or a small glass of sherry or port.) Alcohol abuse also leads to problems at work and to arguments and breakdowns in family life. Alcoholics are psychologically and often physically dependent on alcohol.

A Guide to Sensible Drinking

The government recommend a weekly limit to the number of units of alcohol for men and women

Care workers have a threefold task in relation to alcohol-related problems. The first is one of prevention. This involves your being knowledgeable about sensible drinking and passing on this information to clients. It is perhaps especially important for young people to learn about alcohol, as habits are often formed early. Your second task is one of diagnosis. You need to be able to recognise the early-warning signs when drinking is becoming a problem. The third task is one of treatment and support. This may involve referral to one of the specialist agencies discussed later in this section.

Finding out more: alcohol-related problems

★   There are many leaflets and booklets on the subject of alcohol. These give advice on sensible drinking, provide guidance on recognising early stages of problem drinking, and give sources of information. There are leaflets and booklets specially geared to the needs of various groups, such as women, young people, older people and members of ethnic minorities.

★   The following are sources of information on alcohol and alcohol-related problems.

● The local health promotion department will hold a range of free leaflets; it will also have a library of books that may be borrowed.
● Alcohol Concern is a large national charity with government funding. It is involved in a wide range of activities, including running training courses, producing information, and supporting local groups and activities.

Help for people with alcohol-related problems

Treatment and rehabilitation for people with alcohol-related problems is provided by the NHS, social services, voluntary organisations and the private sector. Under the NHS and Community Care Act, social workers must assess people to decide what services are required and plan and purchase service provision.

Residential and day centres

There are various residential centres throughout the country. Some are private; some are run by voluntary organisations. The addresses can be found from Alcohol Concern or from local **alcohol advisory centres**. The centres work with various treatment programmes, often including group therapy. Following an assessment, social services may pay for treatment in an independently run centre. Day centres may be run by the health and social services or by voluntary organisations.

Hospital treatment

Some NHS hospitals have **detoxification units,** in which patients are monitored in the days of withdrawal from alcohol. This is necessary only in very severe cases of alcohol dependence. (Detoxification can also take place at home with the support of a GP, a nurse and the family.)

The NHS also provides **alcohol treatment units** which offer an alcohol-free environment, social skills training, counselling and support. These may be for in-patients, out-patients or day patients.

Support

Alcoholics Anonymous (AA) is the best-known organisation. It has local groups in most parts of the country. It is a fellowship of recovering alcoholics. The philosophy of AA is one of total abstinence, and members follow a twelve-step plan to recovery. There is a religious aspect to this plan which can be off-putting to some. Although all groups follow the basic philosophy, each local group will have its own atmosphere:

TO DO
Look at the leaflet *That's the Limit*. It is available from local health promotion centres or by writing to the Health Education Authority (address in the appendix). What amount of alcohol do you imagine to be a risk to health? Compare your ideas with the limits suggested. Check your own alcohol intake against the levels set by the government.

TO THINK ABOUT
Do you have any stereotypes about alcoholics which might make it hard for you to recognise that someone has an alcohol problem? What mental picture is conjured up for you by the word 'alcoholic'?

The reality is that there are people with alcohol-related problems of all ages and in all walks of life. Women become alcoholics as well as men, for example, and Asians and Afro-Caribbeans as well as white people.

prospective members could usefully try two or three to find the one which best fits their needs. Anonymity is guaranteed in the AA.

Al-Anon Family Groups is an organisation for families and friends of alcoholics who meet to share their experience, strength and hope. There are over a thousand local groups in the UK and Eire and an extensive range of leaflets and other information is available. Alateen is part of the organisation and meets the needs of young people whose lives are, or have been, affected by a parent or other relative's misuse of alcohol.

Drinkline is a telephone helpline for anyone who needs advice or information about alcohol. The service offers support to people who are worried about their own drinking and to relatives and friends of people who are drinking. Drinkline can also provide information on local sources of help.

Counselling

There are over forty **alcohol advice centres** (also known as **local councils on alcohol**) throughout the country. These provide specialist counselling and advice. The address can be found in *The Phone Book* or by contacting Alcohol Concern.

3.9 Special services for people with drug-related problems

There is a wide range of drugs which affect how people think, feel and behave. Some of these are legal, for example caffeine, alcohol and tobacco; others, such as ecstasy, heroin and cannabis, are illegal. Some, like tranquillisers, are medically prescribed. The drugs vary in their short- and long-term effects but all can be subject to misuse. Many, but not all, drugs cause physical and/or psychological dependence, with accompanying withdrawal effects if the drugs are not taken. The effects of drugs vary from individual to individual and sometimes with different situations. For more information on the effects of various drugs see the leaflet called *Drug and Solvent Misuse* which is available free from the Department of Health.

Most Health Authorities have a department specialising in drug and drug-related problems. This will provide advice and information as well as counselling and treatment. Some also provide free **needle exchanges**. The department may or may not also work with people with alcohol problems.

Outside the health service, there is a national voluntary organisation which provides information on services for people with drug problems. This is *SCODA* – the *Standing Conference on Drug Abuse*. SCODA co-ordinates the work of voluntary organisations working in this area and provides a central source of information. It is also a pressure group, trying to influence the government and to improve the quality of services generally. Several publications are available from SCODA, including a newsletter and a directory of services, nationally and locally. SCODA also sets up meetings for people working in the field. Another voluntary organisation is *ADFAM National*. This provides advice and support for families and friends of people taking drugs. It has a telephone helpline. ADFAM also provides advice, information and training for people working with those with drug problems.

There are also a number of local self-help groups in various parts of the country. SCODA can provide information on local availability.

Residential centres are situated around the country which work to help people come off drugs. These usually have a structured programme of activities including group sessions and individual counselling. SCODA can provide information on these centres, with a brief summary of the approach in each case. Social services departments will pay for treatment following an assessment of the person's needs and financial situation.

There is a national organisation specifically concerned with **solvent abuse** (or 'glue-sniffing'). This is called *Re-Solv*. Re-Solv provides education and information for professionals who might come into contact with young people involved in glue-sniffing. It produces a newsletter and useful publications. It also runs training sessions, helping people to learn to identify the signs of this problem.

Finding out more: help with drug-related problems

★ A useful leaflet from the Department of Health called *Drug and Solvent Abuse* gives information for professionals, parents and others on the effects of drugs and also includes useful addresses.
★ Re-solv publishes a National Directory which is an excellent guide to local and national services provided by the state and by voluntary

The Department of Health publishes information on drugs

organisations. Some are specifically concerned with glue-sniffing and some are more general.

★ The National Drugs Helpline provides free and confidential advice and information on all kinds of problems concerning drugs.

★ The Department of Health publishes a number of leaflets on drugs and solvents.

★ Narcotics Anonymous is a self-help group for people with drug problems.

★ CITA (The Council for Involuntary Tranquilliser Addiction) offers information and support for people who are trying to give up drugs which they have been prescribed. CITA also aims to improve awareness of addiction to tranquillisers.

WORDCHECK

alcohol advisory centres (also known as **local councils on alcohol**) Centres that provide counselling and information.

group therapy A way of exploring personal problems through discussion in a small group with a leader.

detoxification The monitoring of a person with severe alcohol dependency as the patient cuts out all alcohol.

alcohol treatment units NHS centres that help people with alcohol dependency.

needle exchange A place where drug addicts can exchange used syringes for new ones, to minimise the spread of infection.

TO DO

Consider the following clients:

- A woman who has been prescribed tranquillisers and sleeping tablets for some time and would like to stop taking these.
- A parent who suspects that her son is sniffing glue and other solvents.
- A young person addicted to heroin.

Imagine these people are your clients.

- Which national organisations would provide information?
- What local services could help?
- How could you help the clients make use of the services?
- What other support could you offer?

3.10 Help with mental health

The GP is likely to be the first point of contact. He or she may be able to provide some counselling, although many GPs do not personally have the time or the training to offer this. Some surgeries have counsellors or psychiatric nurses and provide individual or group therapy. In cases such as depression, GPs are likely to prescribe drugs, either anti-depressants or tranquillisers. The GP may want to refer the patient to a more specialised service.

Some areas have **mental-health centres**, which act as a kind of gateway for all mental-health services. These are multi-disciplinary, with a number of different workers based at the centre. These might include a psychiatrist, a psychologist, community psychiatric nurses and a social worker. There may also be art therapists and occupational therapists. In other cases, these services might be based at a hospital. In larger towns there may be mental-health centres working with people from particular ethnic backgrounds. The multi-disciplinary team may include a lawyer, to support people where there is an overlap between crime and mental health.

Finding out more: mental health

★ The Department of Health has produced a set of straightforward booklets on mental illness. These are available free by calling the Health Literature Line on 0800 555777 or writing to HMSO Oldham (address in the appendix).

★ *The Mental Health Handbook* by Tony Drew and Madeleine King, 1995 (London: Piatkus) covers all aspects of mental health.

★ MIND produces an excellent series of leaflets on the various mental illnesses. These explain the condition and the symptoms, look at possible causes, describe the various treatments and give sources of further information. The leaflets are:

- *Understanding Anxiety*;
- *Understanding Bereavement*;
- *Understanding Childhood Distress*;
- *Understanding Dementia*;
- *Understanding Depression*;
- *Understanding Eating Distress*;
- *Understanding Manic Depression*;
- *Understanding Mental Illness*;
- *Understanding Phobias and Obsessions*;
- *Understanding Post-Natal Depression*;
- *Understanding Post-Traumatic Stress Disorder*;
- *Understanding Seasonal Affective Disorder*;
- *Understanding Schizophrenia*;
- *Understanding Self-harm*.

★ Young Minds Trust has produced a series of free leaflets on mental health in children and young people.

One of a series of leaflets on mental health produced by the Department of Health

Young Minds is the children's mental health charity

★ There are a number of organisations which provide information on particular mental illnesses. They may also have local groups and put people in touch with each other. The following are two examples:

● *Depressives Anonymous* provides a newsletter, meetings, pen-friends and advice on how to start a local group or information about an existing group.

● The *National Schizophrenia Fellowship* is for people with schizophrenia and also friends and relatives of people suffering from this illness. It provides information, advice and support. There are local groups which meet and sometimes are involved in local projects.

Mental-health professionals

A **psychiatrist** is a doctor who has specialist training in mental health. Some specialise further, perhaps in child psychiatry. People are usually referred to a psychiatrist through their GP. The psychiatrist makes an assessment. Following this, he or she may recommend admission to hospital, or that the patient sees another mental-health worker such as a psychotherapist for individual or group work. Psychiatrists also offer therapy themselves.

A **clinical psychologist** has a degree in psychology and has done further training. Clinical psychologists are involved in the assessment of mental-health problems. They also run groups and work with families and individuals.

Social workers help people with mental-health problems. They provide information and advice. They offer support for individuals and families. Some social workers have extra training in counselling and therapy, and work as therapists with individuals, couples or families. **Family therapy** is a specialised technique for untangling and resolving difficulties in whole families. Social workers also work with groups such as art groups, creative-writing groups and drama groups. They may offer groups for particular people, such as women, or girls who have experienced abuse. Some social services departments run drop-in centres. For people with long-term mental-health problems social services may run hostels, employment schemes and holidays. **Approved social workers** (**ASWs**) are specially trained and have powers to admit people to a psychiatric hospital (see the section on the law and mental illness).

Community psychiatric nurses (**CPNs**) also provide support and counselling for people in the community. They visit at home and work from mental-health or other centres. They can administer drugs.

Hospital care

The doctors and other health workers will try whenever possible to provide care for people with a mental illness in their own homes. Nowadays it is less common than in the past for people to be admitted to a hospital. Even patients who were admitted many years ago are being discharged into the community. However, there are still cases where hospital admission is necessary. Patients who need to go into hospital may go into a psychiatric ward of a district general hospital or into a psychiatric hospital. In a large psychiatric hospital there are usually different wards for different types of illnesses. There are acute wards for patients with short-term illnesses such as depression, and chronic wards for those with longer-term illnesses.

Hospitals provide various sorts of treatments. These include:

- drug treatments, from minor tranquillisers for cases of anxiety to major tranquillisers for problems such as schizophrenia;
- 'talking treatments', such as counselling, group therapy and psycho-therapy;
- electro-convulsive therapy (ECT), for cases of very deep depression;
- behaviour modification – changing people's responses to situations, perhaps by systems of reward and punishment;
- psychosurgery (rarely used, and only as a last resort).

Large psychiatric hospitals have a variety of different staff. Day-to-day care is provided by psychiatric nurses. There are also psychiatrists, psycho-logists and social workers (see earlier). Occupational therapists also work in psychiatric hospitals, helping with rehabilitation. A hospital may also have special staff such as art therapists and drama therapists. These people work with patients, helping them to express their feelings.

Finding out more: mental-health treatments

★ MIND produces a set of pamphlets on some of the treatments for mental illnesses. The pamphlets are:

- *Making Sense of Treatments and Drugs: Anti-Depressants*;
- *Making Sense of Treatments and Drugs: ECT*;
- *Making Sense of Treatments and Drugs: Lithium*;
- *Making Sense of Treatments and Drugs: Major Tranquillizers*;
- *Making Sense of Treatments and Drugs: Minor Tranquillizers*.

The leaflets describe the treatments, side-effects and alternatives.

Other sources of care

There are also services provided outside the NHS – by voluntary organisations, or privately. *MIND* (The Mental Health Charity) is the main voluntary organisation concerned with mental health. At the national level, it campaigns to promote the rights of people with mental illnesses and to counter the stigma attached to mental illness. It produces a large number of excellent leaflets on various aspects of mental health. Further, it can provide legal and other advice from the national office. There are also some 200 local MIND groups. The services provided vary from area to area, but may include drop-in centres, housing, social groups, employment projects and befriending schemes.

The *Samaritans* are another resource for people with mental-health problems. The Samaritans provide a confidential, 24-hours-a-day/7-days-a-week service. People can phone or visit the local office.

A different kind of listening and support is offered by **counsellors** and **psychotherapists**. Although counselling and psychotherapy are similar and overlap a great deal, there may be slight differences in emphasis. It is likely that a psychotherapist will concentrate on the client's past, especially their experiences as a child in the family. A counsellor will deal more with current problems and issues.

There are various different types of training which counsellors and psychotherapists may have had, but there are no legally required qualifications. The training consists of diplomas and master's degrees in counselling and psychotherapy, and suitably qualified people can apply for membership of the British Association for Counselling (BAC). Private therapy will cost £20–£30 for a 50-minute session. It is usually weekly and often long-term. It is not uncommon for people to see a therapist regularly for a year or more.

Sometimes it is possible to get therapy within the NHS, in which case it will be free. MIND may also provide a free counselling service locally. There may be other voluntary organisations which provide a counselling service, perhaps for particular groups such as young people or women. Another way to get free counselling or therapy is from students in training. It is worth contacting a local college to see whether this is possible.

Although counselling has something of a white middle-class image, it can help anyone who needs to talk through their problems. In some areas there are services specially tailored to the needs of people from ethnic minorities.

Finding out more: counselling and psychotherapy

★   There are several leaflets and many books which give information on counselling and psychotherapy:

- *Who Can I Talk To? The User Guide to Therapy and Counselling* by Judy Cooper and Jenny Lewis, published in 1995 by Headway, provides information on the various therapies and counselling services available in the UK;
- *Counselling and You* is a leaflet produced by the British Association for Counselling;
- The British Association for Psychotherapists produces leaflets explaining psychotherapy.

★   For information on the names of counsellors and counselling and psychothcrapy organisations, contact the British Association for Counselling. Another organisation involved in therapy, for women only, is the Women's Therapy Centre.

Therapeutic communities

Around the country, there are a number of therapeutic communities run by voluntary organisations. One example is the communities run by the *Richmond Fellowship*. The communities provide a supportive environment in which people help each other, with back-up provided by trained staff. There will usually be group meetings to discuss day-to-day decisions and to allow people to talk through their feelings and problems. State funding may be available for someone who would benefit from this kind of support. Information on therapeutic communities is available from MIND.

Finally, there may be day centres, drop-in centres and various groups provided by people with mental illnesses. These may be run by social services departments or by a local MIND group.

WORDCHECK

mental-health centres Gateways for people with mental-health problems who are seeking help.

psychiatrist A doctor who specialises in mental health.

psychologist Someone with a degree in psychology, involved usually in assessment.

community psychiatric nurse Someone who provides support and nursing for people with mental-health problems who are living in the community.

occupational therapist Someone who helps people with disabilities to live a normal life, teaching necessary skills and providing special equipment.

family therapy A way of exploring relationships and problems between members of a family, all of whom are involved in the therapy.

acute ward A short-stay ward in a hospital.

chronic ward A longer-stay ward in a hospital.

group therapy A way of exploring personal problems through discussion in a small group with a leader.

electro-convulsive therapy (ECT) Treatment for severe depression which involves passing an electric current through the brain.

behaviour modification Treatment to change behaviour: it involves systems of reward and punishment.

psychosurgery Treatment for severe mental illness, very rarely used, which involves surgery on the brain.

stigma Something which sets a person apart and causes feelings of embarrassment or shame.

voluntary organisation An organisation which has not been set up by a government body and which does not aim to make a profit.

therapeutic community A residential centre which can help people come to terms with their feelings and solve emotional and psychological problems.

approved social worker A social worker with extra training who is involved with admitting people to psychiatric hospitals.

Finding out more: therapeutic communities

★ The Richmond Fellowship can provide information on the therapeutic communities it runs.

★ Another source of information on therapeutic communities is *A Directory of Therapeutic Communities*, available from the Association of Therapeutic Communities.

The law and mental illness

This mostly concerns hospitalisation of people with a mental illness. By far the majority of people with a mental illness who are in hospital are there as **informal patients**. This means that they have gone into hospital voluntarily. They have the same legal rights as someone in hospital for treatment for a physical illness. Informal patients can leave the hospital if they want to, and they do not have to accept treatment. About 95 per cent of patients in psychiatric hospitals are informal patients. The remaining 5 per cent are **formal patients** who are in hospital under one or other section of the 1983 Mental Health Act. They cannot leave when they please, and they have lost some other rights as well.

There are four sections of the Mental Health Act which are especially relevant when people are so mentally ill that it is necessary to admit them compulsorily to hospital. This may be done because it is thought that they are a danger to themselves – that they are likely to try to commit suicide or in some other way harm themselves. Sometimes mentally ill people become violent and are a danger to others. Such people may not consider themselves to be mentally ill, and may refuse any help or treatment. This section explains how the law can be used in such cases. The law on mental health is powerful since it gives social workers and doctors the right to take away people's freedom and to force people to go into psychiatric hospitals. It is important that it is not abused. There is a safeguard with the **Mental Health Review Tribunal (MHRT)** which allows patients to have their cases reviewed.

Section 4

Section 4 of the Mental Health Act is concerned with admission to hospital in emergency cases. The application for admission is made by a social worker or a close relative. The social worker must be an **approved social worker (ASW)**, who has completed extra training in this area of work. The social worker or relative must have seen the person in the last 24 hours. Then it is necessary for a doctor to agree that there is an 'urgent necessity' for the patient to be admitted and that to wait would cause 'undesirable delay'.

Admission is for 72 hours only. At the end of that period, the patient may stay in hospital as an informal patient. Alternatively, the patient may leave, unless the doctor makes an application to keep the patient in hospital under Section 3 for a longer period for treatment.

Section 2

Under Section 2 of the Mental Health Act a patient can be admitted to hospital for a maximum of 28 days. Again the application must be made by an approved social worker or the nearest relative. The social worker or relative must have seen the patient in the last 14 days. Two doctors must agree that the person needs to be in hospital and is otherwise a danger to himself or herself or to someone else. The patient can apply to a Mental Health Review Tribunal within 14 days of being admitted, as a means of having the case reviewed.

In certain cases, the patient may leave hospital before the 28 days are up. This can happen if someone is discharged by their doctor, or by the hospital management or the MHRT. The nearest relative can also discharge the patient, but must give 72 hours' notice to the hospital. If the doctor does not agree with the patient leaving, the doctor can overrule the relative.

At the end of the 28 days, the patient can leave, or stay as an informal patient, unless the doctor makes an application to keep the patient in hospital under Section 3 for a longer period of treatment.

Section 3

Section 3 of the Act allows a person to be kept in hospital for six months in the first instance. This can be extended for a further six months. After that, the extensions are for one year at a time. Two doctors must agree that hospitalisation is necessary in the interests of the safety of the individual or of others. Patients can apply to the MHRT once in the first six months and once in the second six months. After that the case is reviewed annually.

Section 5

Section 5 of the Act is concerned with people already in hospital as informal patients. A doctor can prevent an informal patient from leaving the hospital for 72 hours by telling the hospital management that an application for a section should be made. A nurse can keep someone in hospital for up to six hours or until the arrival of a doctor with the authority to keep the patient. An application can be made for a longer stay under Section 3 of the Act.

Discharge from hospital

The Mental Health (Patients in the Community) Act 1995 allows for 'supervised discharge' of patients who are considered ready to leave hospital but who may still be a risk to themselves or others. Under this legislation, the patient can be placed under the supervision of a unit providing specialised care in the community. A supervised discharge is for six months initially, can be extended for a further six months, and then is renewed annually if necessary.

Representation at a tribunal

Patients are allowed to have someone else to represent them at a Mental Health Review Tribunal. This can be anyone, but it is best to have someone who understands and can use the law on mental health. Both MIND and the Law Society can recommend someone with special expertise in this area. If a solicitor is used, a patient with a low income can have free representation under the legal aid scheme.

WORDCHECK

informal patient A patient who is in hospital voluntarily and not under any part of the mental-health legislation.

Mental Health Review Tribunal A body which reviews cases of people admitted to psychiatric hospitals under the 1983 Mental Health Act.

approved social worker A social worker with extra training who is involved with admitting people to psychiatric hospitals.

Finding out more: mental health and the law

★ MIND produces a set of Rights Guides designed to help mental health services users, their relatives and caring workers understand the law on mental health. The titles in the series are:

- *Rights Guide 1: Civil Admission to Hospital*;
- *Rights Guide 2: Mental Health and the Police*;
- *Rights Guide 3: Consent to Medical Treatment*;
- *Rights Guide 4: Discharge from Hospital*;
- *Rights Guide 5: Mental Health and the Courts*.

★ See also *Law for Social Workers* (fourth edition, 1995) by Hugh Brayne and Gerry Martin, published by Blackstone Press.

CASE STUDY

Janet lives alone. Over the last six months her behaviour has become increasingly bizarre and erratic. She has talked to neighbours about voices which tell her to buy a gun. Her relatives are concerned and have contacted social services. Janet would not open the door to the social worker on the two occasions he visited.

1 How could the law be used in this example? Which are the relevant sections? Which professionals need to be involved?

2 Apart from using the law, how else could Janet be helped? What treatments might be appropriate? Which mental-health workers could get involved? Which other services might be needed?

3.11 Private health care

Some people choose to pay for private health care. It may be that they feel they will receive a better standard of care than they would get in the NHS. The differences tend not to be in the quality of medical care received, however, but in the 'frills' – the availability of private rooms, telephones, and so on. Another reason people choose private health care is that there are sometimes long waiting lists in the NHS for certain – usually, but not always, non-urgent – types of treatment. One example here is hip-replacement operations: around a third of these are carried out privately.

There are now about two hundred private hospitals around the country and about three thousand 'pay beds' in NHS hospitals. The majority of people paying privately do so through one or another of the private insurance companies. Two of the largest are *British United Provident Association (BUPA)* and *Private Patient Plan (PPP)*. About two million people subscribe to private insurance schemes. Since a lot of subscriptions are for families, this means that about six million people have private cover.

There are limits on what private insurance will cover. Some companies will not take people over 65 as new subscribers, for example. Someone with a disability or long-standing illness can join, but he or she will not be insured for any treatment of an illness they had at the time of joining. This also applies to any condition *related* to an existing illness. Likely exclusions include:

- seeing a GP privately;
- routine health checks;
- out-patient drugs;
- cosmetic treatments;
- convalescence;
- maternity care;
- items such as glasses or wheelchairs;
- routine dental work;
- any HIV-related treatment within (say) five years of joining.

There are also limits to the amount which can be claimed. Private health insurance works best for basically well people who might need minor treatment for an acute short-term illness or injury.

Finding out more: private health care

★ For more information on private health care, contact The Medical Advisory Service. This organisation can give information on all health resources, not just private ones.

TO DO

Contact at least two private health insurance schemes. Find out the costs.

Look carefully at the small print to see exactly what cover is given and what is excluded. Compare the two schemes, and make notes on their strengths and weaknesses.

3.12 Complementary medicine

The kind of medicine offered within the NHS is only one approach to medicine. It tends to concentrate on physical symptoms and to rely heavily on drugs and surgery to treat symptoms. Some people are not happy with this approach or have found it ineffective for a particular illness or condition. Alternative approaches do exist. There are many types of **complementary medicine** and only a few of the more common practices are described here.

Acupuncture

Acupuncture is an ancient Chinese art. It involves needles being placed in particular parts of the body. The needles may be left for seconds only or for a longer period such as half an hour. The needles may have electricity passed through them or they may be manipulated by hand. Although it sounds as if it must be painful, users say it is not.

Finding out more: acupuncture

★ The British Medical Acupuncture Society has a list of members who are conventional doctors and who also practise acupuncture. People seeking treatment must be referred by their own GP.
★ The British Acupuncture Association has members who are not conventionally qualified doctors.

Osteopathy

Osteopathy is the most popular type of alternative treatment in the UK. Osteopaths take a holistic approach, looking at the whole person: their personality and lifestyle, as well as symptoms such as pain. The treatment involves physical manipulation of the spine and joints.

Finding out more: osteopathy

★ The General Council and Register of Osteopaths can provide information.

Chiropractic

This is similar to osteopathy. It is gaining in popularity and in other parts of the world is more commonly practised than osteopathy. Like osteopathy, it involves physical manipulation of the back and limbs. Chiropractors are more likely to use more sudden thrusting movements, whereas osteopaths combine their treatment with massage.

Finding out more: chiropractic

★ The British Chiropractic Association can provide information.

The General Council and Register of Osteopaths has information leaflets on osteopathy

The British Homoeopathic Association provides information on homeopathy

Homeopathy

This is another holistic approach to medicine. The homeopath will spend a relatively long time finding out about the patient. Life history, personality and lifestyle will be taken into account in making a decision on the best treatment. There are two main principles in homeopathy. The first is that like can cure like, and that the smallest dose of a treatment is the most effective. Secondly, symptoms are seen positively: as part of the body's attempt to cure itself. Homeopaths do not treat people with infectious diseases or injuries or cancer – they are most popular in treating conditions such as allergies, pains in joints and stomach problems.

Some doctors who practise within the NHS have also trained in one of the alternative treatments. These doctors may be able to offer treatment within the NHS. Homeopathy can be obtained within the health service and there are hospitals working to these principles which can take NHS patients. Homeopathic medicines can be bought at chemists and health shops.

Finding out more: homeopathy

★ The British Homeopathic Association provides information on homeopathy and encourages further developments in homeopathy.

Aromatherapy

Aromatherapy involves the use of oils to improve health and well-being by massage, inhalation, compresses and baths. Aromatherapy is most often used as a treatment for stress and anxiety.

Finding out more: aromatherapy

★ The following organisations will send information on practitioners in return for a stamped addressed envelope:

- The International Federation of Aromatherapists;
- International Society of Professional Aromatherapists;
- The Register for Qualified Aromatherapists.

The Alexander Technique

The Alexander Technique teaches people to use their bodies more efficiently in all everyday movements and positions. People gain in poise and balance and avoid pain, strain and injury. The technique has been especially popular with actors, musicians and horse-riders.

Finding Out More: The Alexander Technique

★ The Society of Teachers of the Alexander Technique (STAT) provides information, a booklist and lists of practising teachers.

The Bristol Cancer Help Centre

The Bristol Cancer Help Centre provides an holistic approach for people with cancer and their carers. The centre provides support for people in all stages of cancer and is a source of information on all aspects of cancer. The centre uses a range of complementary therapies to promote general health and well-being and to help with symptoms and the side-effects of treatment. For more information, contact the centre at the address given in the appendix.

Choosing a practitioner

There is no law controlling complementary medical practice. Anyone, without any qualifications, can set themselves up as a healer. So prospective patients need to be cautious. It is worth checking that the practitioner is registered with the appropriate professional body and has training and qualifications.

Finding out more: complementary medicine

★ *The A–Z of Complementary and Alternative Therapies* is published by MIND (1995) and gives details of over 40 therapies with suggestions for further reading and contact addresses.

★ The Alternative Health Information Bureau is a computerised resource centre for holistic health care which brings together research into alternative and complementary medicines around the world.

★ Look in a library for *The Handbook of Alternative and Complementary Medicine* by Stephen Fulder (ed.), published by Oxford University Press, 1996.

WORDCHECK

alternative or **complementary medicine** Forms of treatment other than Western or orthodox medicine.
osteopath Someone who treats injuries by manipulating the spine and joints.
homeopath Someone who practises alternative healing, by treating the whole person with small doses of medicine.
acupuncturist Someone who treats people by inserting needles into the body.
chiropractor Someone who treats injuries by manipulation of the back and limbs.
aromatherapy The use of oils to improve health and well-being by massage, inhalation, compresses and baths.

The Bristol Cancer Help Centre uses a range of complementary therapies in its holistic approach to people with cancer

---

TO DO

1 Find out about practitioners of complementary medicine in your area. *Yellow Pages* is a useful source of information, or the organisations listed could be used.

2 Conduct a survey to find out how many people have consulted an alternative practitioner. Without being too personal, try to find out their reasons for doing so. Were they happy with the treatment? Would they recommend the healer?

4 Money

This chapter looks at ways in which people are entitled to financial help. This is an important area of need as money is the means to so much in life. Poverty affects physical health and reduces people's opportunities.

Most of the information in this chapter concerns social security benefits. The system is complicated and no one – probably not even the people who work in the social security offices – could be expected to know everything about all the benefits. But it is important that people in the caring professions have at least an *outline* knowledge of what people can claim, and certainly that they know how to find out what is available.

Millions of pounds of benefits go unclaimed each year. One of the main reasons for this is ignorance. People are not aware that the benefits exist, or that they would be eligible for a benefit. This is where you can help, by tactfully finding out whether your clients are receiving all the benefits they are entitled to. Another reason people do not claim benefits is that they are frightened of all the form-filling and the questions they might have to answer. Your support might be welcomed. It is not necessary to be an expert to accompany someone to the benefit office or to help with filling in a form. Some people, especially older people, feel that benefits are a form of charity and they would feel ashamed to claim. They need convincing that the welfare benefits are their right. They have paid into the system through taxes and national insurance. Even someone who has not paid tax through work will have paid tax on things they have bought.

Social security benefits: some general principles

As has been mentioned, the bulk of this chapter is concerned with social security benefits. It is mainly divided in terms of various types of people and the benefits they might be entitled to. However, there are some benefits which people can get in many different situations. These are described first and then referred to throughout the later sections.

In understanding the benefits system, a few general principles will help. Firstly, benefits are divided into those which are means-tested and those which are not. When a **means-tested benefit** is claimed, the income and savings of the person will be looked at. Only people who have incomes and savings below set levels qualify for the benefit. The main benefits which are means-tested are Income Support, Housing Benefit and Family Credit. The income-based part of Jobseeker's Allowance is also means-tested.

Secondly, some benefits are **contributory**. This means that only people who have paid the right amount of national insurance contributions will be able to claim the benefit. Many people think that everyone gets the retirement pension, but this is not so. It is only paid to people who have qualified through their own or their husband's contributions whilst in work. The contributory benefits include the retirement pension, the contributory part of Jobseeker's Allowance and the widows' benefits. Statutory sick pay and statutory maternity pay are also contributory.

Some benefits, however, are neither means-tested nor contributory. This is the case with Child Benefit which is paid to all families with children.

Most benefits are paid according to rules which have been set by Parliament. A few benefits, however, are **discretionary**. This means that the officers assess the claimant's case and decide whether or not the benefit should be given. This is the case for some of the payments from the Social Fund.

The rates at which benefits are paid change each April, and occasionally at other times too. This presents a problem when writing about benefits. In describing the benefits I have, in the main, left out the actual amounts, since these will have changed by the time this book is published. An exception to this is in the examples. Here I wanted to show the kinds of payments which can be expected. The amounts shown relate to the year 1996–97. They can be updated by reference to the sources listed in *Finding out more: benefits*.

Credits and home responsibilities protection

When people do not pay national insurance contributions through their work, there are gaps in their contribution record. However, in a large number of circumstances, people can be 'credited' with contributions. People can get **credits** when they are:

- signing on as unemployed;
- being covered by a sickness certificate;
- receiving Invalid Care Allowance;
- studying on certain training courses;
- receiving maternity pay;
- retired under age 65 (men only);
- receiving Family Credit or Disability Working Allowance and not earning enough to pay contributions;
- looking after a child and receiving Child Benefit;
- caring for someone with a disability.

In the last two situations credits cover a year and are known as **home responsibilities protection**.

The exact rules concerning credits and they way they entitle people to claim particular benefits are very complicated and you should consult someone at the Benefits Agency or get more details from one of the books listed below. In some cases credits are automatically given; in others they must be claimed.

Advice on benefits

Some local authorities provide a **welfare rights unit** to help people with advice and information on benefits. There may also be a local **law centre** which offers free legal and welfare advice. **Trade Union and Unemployed Workers Centres** offer advice to unemployed people and others on their entitlement to benefits. All areas have **Citizens' Advice Bureaux (CABs)** which give free advice in this area. Sometimes the CAB will help with appeals on benefits. There may also be a local *Child Poverty Action Group*. **Claimants Unions** have been set up in some areas: information about these is available from the Federation of Claimants Unions. The Benefits Agency can also provide information on benefits.

Finding out more: benefits

★ The Child Poverty Action Group produces two excellent and detailed guides to benefits. These are updated each April, when the majority of changes are made to the benefits system. The books are:

- *National Welfare Benefits Handbook*;
- *Rights Guide to Non-Means-Tested Benefits*.

★ The Department of Social Security produces a large number of leaflets explaining the various benefits. These are very well produced and most are easy to understand. They range from brief leaflets which give an outline of benefits – to help people find out whether the benefit is worth claiming – to very detailed and comprehensive booklets containing all the rules concerning a benefit. The leaflets are free and are available in Benefits Agency offices, libraries and post offices.

★ The following books provide information for particular client groups. Each is updated annually.

- *Disability Rights Handbook*, published by the Disability Alliance;
- *Unemployment and Training Rights Handbook*, published by the Unemployment Unit;
- *Guide to Training and Benefits for Young People*, published by Youthaid;
- *Your Rights*, published by Age Concern.

WORDCHECK

means-tested benefit A benefit awarded to some and not to others, according to the individual client's income and savings.

contributory benefit A benefit payable to someone who has paid enough national insurance contributions.

discretionary benefit A benefit awarded to some and not to others, the decision being taken by an official according to the merits of the individual case.

law centre A centre which provides free legal advice.

4.1 Income Support

Income Support is a benefit for people who are not working full-time, have a low income and who do not have to be available for work. This includes men aged 60–65, single parents and carers. People in these categories can, if they wish, claim Jobseeker's Allowance instead, providing they are available for work and prepared to actively seek work (see section 4.6).

Entitlement

People on Income Support may have no other income at all, or they may have income from maintenance or other benefits or from a part-time job. In most cases, other income is taken into account in deciding how much benefit will be paid. Another qualification for Income Support concerns savings. People cannot claim Income Support if they have more than £8000 in savings. People with savings, but less than this amount, will find that their benefit is reduced (see below).

The amount of Income Support a person will get is worked out by looking at any income coming in and comparing this to the amount Parliament has decided people are entitled to, known as the **applicable amount**. The amount paid is the balance between these two amounts of money.

As mentioned above, people with savings over £8000 cannot receive Income Support. People with savings between £3000 and £8000 will have some money deducted from the benefit: the deduction is £1 each week for every £250 or part of £250. If the benefit officers suspect that someone has deliberately got rid of their savings in order to claim benefit, this person can be treated as if he or she still has the savings.

Income is counted *after* tax and national insurance deductions. Pensions and earnings count as income, as do certain social security benefits: Child Benefit, for example, is counted in calculating Income Support. Not all income is counted, however. The following are ignored:

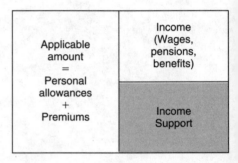

Income Support = applicable amount – income

- Attendance Allowance;
- Mobility Allowance;
- Social Fund payments;
- interest from savings;
- expenses from voluntary work;
- £5 from earnings, or £15 if the person is a lone parent or has a disability;
- £4 from rent paid by a sub-tenant.

Allowances and premiums

As shown in the diagram on page 70, there are two parts to the amount of money decided by Parliament. These are the **personal allowances**, which are based on the number and ages of people in the family; and the **premiums**, which are based on certain aspects of the person's situation. The premiums are supposed to reflect special needs and additional expenses. A personal allowance is paid for each member of the household (a couple receive a different amount). The rates vary according to age.

Premiums are paid *on top of* the personal allowances. There are eight different premiums. Each person may receive *one only* of the following:

- pensioner premium;
- disability premium;
- higher pensioner premium;
- lone-parent premium (people claiming before April 1998).

If someone is eligible for more than one, he or she will receive the *higher* premium only.

One or more of the following premiums may be received *as well*, however:

- carer premium;
- family premium;
- disabled child premium;
- severe disability premium.

For example, a family who has a child with a disability would receive two premiums: the family premium and the disabled child premium. The details of entitlement to the premiums are given below.

Pensioner premium

The pensioner premium is paid at two different rates according to age. There is a lower rate for people aged 60–74 and an enhanced rate for people aged 75–79. Only one partner in a couple has to be older for the couple to receive the enhanced rate.

Disability premium

This is paid to people under 60 who receive one of the following benefits:

- Attendance Allowance;
- Disability Living Allowance;
- Disability Working Allowance;
- Severe Disablement Allowance;
- Incapacity Benefit (paid at the long-term rate).

It is also paid to people who are registered blind or have an NHS invalid trike or private car allowance because of disability.

Higher pensioner premium

This is paid to people aged 80 and over; and to people between 60 and 79 who have a disability.

Lone-parent premium

This is paid to men or women who are caring for a child and who have no partner, providing they claim Income Support before 1998. The premium is not payable for people claiming Income Support after April 1998.

Carer premium

This is for people caring for another person, who receive the Invalid Care Allowance. Others can receive the premium if they would qualify for the Invalid Care Allowance were it not for another benefit they are getting instead.

Family premium

All families with dependent children receive this premium. This includes lone parents, who therefore receive two premiums.

Disabled child premium

This is paid for each child who receives the Disability Living Allowance, or who is registered blind.

Severe disability premium

People qualify for this if they meet all of the following criteria:

- receive an Attendance Allowance or the middle or higher rates of the Disability Living Allowance;
- have no one living with them who is a non-dependent aged 18 or over;
- have no carer who receives Invalid Care Allowance.

Mortgage Interest Payments

People on income support can get help with paying a mortgage for the house in which they live. See Chapter 2 for more details about this.

EXAMPLE: INCOME SUPPORT

Jane is a lone parent with a daughter, Olivia, aged 4. Jane herself is 28. They live in a rented house and Jane has no income other than Child Benefit. She is eligible for Income Support and began claiming in 1996. She receives:

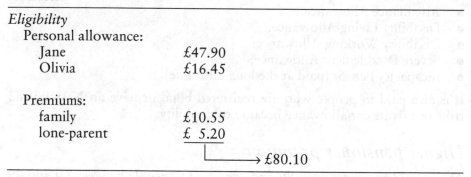

Eligibility		
Personal allowance:		
Jane	£47.90	
Olivia	£16.45	
Premiums:		
family	£10.55	
lone-parent	£ 5.20	
	└──────→ £80.10	

The Child Benefit and One-Parent Benefit count as income and are taken off the amount to be paid as Income Support.

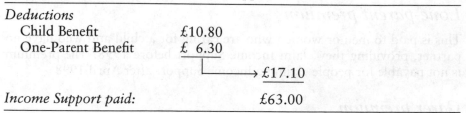

Deductions		
Child Benefit	£10.80	
One-Parent Benefit	£ 6.30	
	└──────→ £17.10	
Income Support paid:	£63.00	

Jane's total income will therefore be £80.10 (the Income Support plus the two benefits), which will have to cover everything for Olivia and herself except rent and council tax. Help with these are available to Jane through Housing Benefit and Council Tax Benefit.

4.2 Young people and benefits

In September 1988, the government decided that 16- and 17-year-olds should not be able to claim benefits. The idea was that they should be in full-time education, in work or on a training scheme. This caused great hardship for some young people and led to the increase in homeless young people begging on the streets of towns such as London.

Some exceptions to the rule that people must be 18 to claim benefits have been introduced. In some circumstances, young people are entitled to claim for a short period of time, provided they are registered for a job or a place on a training scheme. This is known as the **child benefit extension period**. The 'special circumstances' apply if the person:

- is a parent responsible for a child;
- is so severely disabled (mentally or physically) that they would be unlikely to get a job in the next 12 months;
- has no living parent or guardian;
- is living away from parents who are unable to provide because they are in prison, chronically ill or mentally or physically disabled, or who are unable to come to Britain because of the nationality laws;
- is a refugee learning English to improve employment prospects;
- is living away from home because of estrangement or abuse;
- used to be in the care of the local authority and is living away from home through necessity.

There are other circumstances in which a young person may be eligible for benefit at any time. These affect:

- single parents;
- people who are caring for a child because the parents are ill or away;
- people who are looking after a member of the family who is ill;
- people who are receiving an Invalid Care Allowance or caring for someone receiving an Attendance Allowance;
- students with disabilities;
- blind people;
- young women who are pregnant or who have just given birth;
- young people who are incapable of work because of a disability.

Finally, the Secretary of State for Social Security has the discretion to allow Income Support to be paid to prevent 'severe hardship'. This tends only to be for a short period of time. People seeking emergency accommodation in shelters are automatically considered under this rule.

WORDCHECK

Social Fund A fund which can provide loans and grants for buying larger items or in times of crisis.

premium A part of Income Support, for people with extra needs such as older people or one-parent families.

personal allowance The other part of Income Support, calculated on the basis of age.

4.3 The Social Fund

The Social Fund is meant to help people with larger and exceptional payments – the kind it is hard to plan for and which cannot be paid for out of weekly benefit payments. There are two parts to the Social Fund, making *discretionary* and *non-discretionary* payments.

The **non-discretionary payments** are made according to rules set down in law: people receive the payment if they meet the criteria. They receive a set amount decided by Parliament. This type of payment is made for funerals and for maternity costs. Cold Weather Payments are also made on a non-discretionary basis.

The **discretionary payments** are of three types: Community Care Grants, Budgeting Loans and Crisis Loans. With these, each case is assessed by a Social Fund officer who decides whether a payment should be made. The officer can use his or her discretion in each case. The discretionary payments are also **cash-limited**. This means that each office is allocated a certain amount of money each year and cannot spend any more. The Social Fund officer must decide each case bearing this in mind.

Non-discretionary payments

Funeral payments

Funeral payments can be claimed by people who are getting Income Support, Income-based Jobseeker's Allowance, Housing Benefit or Family Credit. The payment consists of up to £500 for a funeral director's fees and extra amounts to cover certain costs including, for example, the cost of the burial or cremation and an amount of money for flowers. In deciding how much to pay, the Social Fund officer will take account of any money available to pay for a funeral. This includes any insurance policies and money from the dead person's estate. Savings over £500 belonging to the person responsible for the funeral are also taken into account. For people over 60 the amount is £1000.

Maternity expenses

Maternity expenses can be claimed by people on Family Credit or Income Support who are expecting a baby or who have just had a baby. The payment is £100. If the claimant has savings over £500, the payment is reduced by £1 for every pound of capital over £500.

Cold Weather Payment

The **Cold Weather Payment** is paid in a period of exceptionally cold weather. This means that the average temperature for each day is at or below 0 degrees Celsius for a period of seven days running. People who qualify are those on Income Support and receiving one of the following premiums: pensioner premium, disability premium, higher pensioner premium, severe disability premium and disabled child premium. People with children under five also qualify. The payment is £8.50 for each week of cold weather.

Discretionary payments

Community Care Grants

Community Care Grants do not have to be repaid. However the Community Care Grant is a discretionary and cash-limited payment. The Social Fund officer will therefore make a decision based on the needs of the people applying and the amount of money remaining in the fund. Payments can be made in a number of circumstances. People who are moving out of residential care, for example a hospital for people with learning disabilities, can receive help with costs such as fuel connections or essential items like a cooker. Payments can be made to help people stay in the community, for example to meet the costs of minor repairs or to buy essential furniture. Grants can also be made to help with exceptional pressures on families caused by disability, chronic sickness or major family changes. In urgent situations, travel expenses can be met, for example to go to a funeral or to visit a sick relative.

Budgeting Loans

Budgeting Loans are paid to people who have been on Income Support or income-related Jobseeker's Allowance for at least 26 weeks. They are again discretionary and cash-limited. Since the payment is a loan, the Social Fund officer will include assessment of the person's ability to pay in the decision as to whether or not to give a loan. The loan will be repaid by deductions from benefit. No interest is charged on the loan. Budgeting Loans are for large items which cannot be paid for out of weekly benefit, such as a new cooker or a bed. The loan can be between £30 and £1000.

Crisis Loans

People do not have to be on benefits to receive a **Crisis Loan**. People who are excluded from claiming a Crisis Loan are:

- those in hospital, nursing homes or residential care homes;
- prisoners;
- those living in convents or monasteries;
- those in full-time education.

Crisis Loans are for emergency needs, for example following a flood or a fire. They are given where money is needed to prevent risk to health and safety.

4.4 Housing Benefit

Housing Benefit is paid to people on a low income who rent their home. It can be claimed by people in full-time work, as well as by those people living on Income Support, income-based Jobseeker's Allowance or other benefits. It is paid by the local authority housing department. Housing Benefit cannot be claimed by people with savings over £16 000. People with savings over £3000 but less than £16 000 will have the amount of Housing Benefit they claim reduced. Every £250 will count as income of £1 a week.

Calculating Housing Benefit involves a number of steps.

Step 1: the rent

The first step is to assess the amount of *rent* which can be claimed. The maximum is 100 per cent of the rent.

There are rules about what counts as rent. For example, fuel charges or water rates cannot be included. Deductions are made where non-dependants share the house.

In most cases the local authority must refer a claim for rent to the rent officer who will make a decision about the maximum rent which can be paid. This decision will be based on several factors: a comparison between the rent claimed and rents charged locally and whether the accommodation is seen as being too big or too expensive. People under 60 who live alone in rented accomodation are eligible only for benefit equivalent to the average rent of a room in a shared house.

Step 2: money coming in

The second step is to look at *capital and income*. As described above, £1 of income a week is assumed for each £250 of savings between £3000 and £16 000. Income is counted after deductions for tax and national insurance.

Some income is ignored:

- Attendance Allowance;
- Mobility Allowance;
- Social Fund payments;
- actual income from savings;
- of earnings, £5 for a single person, £10 for a couple, £15 for a person with a disability;
- £4 income from a sub-tenant;
- the care component of the Disability Living Allowance.

Step 3: applicable amounts

The third step is to consider the *applicable amount* for the person or family. This is calculated in the same way as for Income Support, with personal allowances and premiums (see section 4.1).

If the claimant's income is the same as or below the total applicable amount, the rent will be paid in full. This would be the case for someone on Income Support. For people with a higher income, a reduction is made. The amount paid is reduced by 65 per cent of the difference between the income and the applicable amount. In other words, the maximum Housing Benefit is reduced by 65 pence for every £1 over the applicable amount.

HELP WITH YOUR RENT

HOUSING BENEFIT

Housing Benefit helps people on low incomes pay their rent

EXAMPLE 1

Martin is single and unemployed. He is 26 and receives a Jobseeker's Allowance of £42.45. He rents a room in a shared house and pays a rent of £40 a week.

The applicable amount for him is £42.45 a week. This is the same as his income, so he gets all his rent paid in Housing Benefit.

EXAMPLE 2

Mr and Mrs Wong are aged 62 and 65. They have an income of £102.10 a week from a pension. They live in a council flat and pay £50.00 a week in rent. They have savings of £4000.

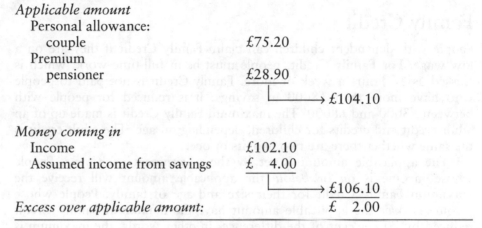

Applicable amount		
Personal allowance:		
couple	£75.20	
Premium		
pensioner	£28.90	
		→ £104.10
Money coming in		
Income	£102.10	
Assumed income from savings	£ 4.00	
		→ £106.10
Excess over applicable amount:		£ 2.00

The money coming in is *higher* than the applicable amount, so the Housing Benefit is reduced by 65 pence for each £1 above the applicable amount. In this case, this is £1.30.

Full rent	£50.00
Reduction	£ 1.30
Housing benefit paid:	£48.70

WORDCHECK

Social Fund A fund which can provide loans and grants for buying larger items or in times of crisis.

discretionary benefit A benefit awarded to some and not to others, the decision being taken by an official according to the merits of the individual case.

cash-limited Dependent on the money available, as in the case of some parts of the Social Fund – a certain sum of money is available initially; once this has been spent, no more payments can be made.

applicable amount The amount of money a household is calculated to need: the income is assessed and compared with this to decide how much benefit is to be paid.

premium A part of Income Support, for people with extra needs such as older people or one-parent families.

personal allowance The other part of Income Support, calculated on the basis of age.

4.5 Benefits for families in work

Child Benefit

All parents are entitled to **Child Benefit**. This is paid for each child, with a higher amount for the first child. Lone parents receiving Child Benefit before April 1998 also get One-Parent Benefit, which is £6.30. This is the same whatever the number of children. From April 1998, new lone parents do not receive this additional benefit. Child Benefit lasts until the child is 16, or 19 if in full-time education.

Family Credit

People with dependent children can claim **Family Credit** if they are on a low wage. For Family Credit, people must be in full-time work, which is classed as 16 hours a week or more. Family Credit is not paid to people who have more than £8000 in savings. It is reduced for people with between £3000 and £8000. The maximum Family Credit is made up of an adult credit and credits for children, depending on age. The adult credit is the same whether there are two parents or one.

The applicable amount is set by the government each year. People whose income is *on or below* the applicable amount will receive the maximum Family Credit for their size and age of family. People whose income is *over* the applicable amount have the maximum Family Credit reduced by 70 per cent of the difference. In other words, the maximum is reduced by 70 pence for every £1 someone earns over the applicable amount, £75.20. The income considered is the net wages; Child Benefit is not counted. In some cases the costs of child care can be taken into account. Where someone has savings of between £3000 and £8000, £1 of income per week is assumed for each £250.

Family Credit is a **passport benefit**, giving automatic entitlement to some other benefits. These are free prescriptions, free dental care, free sight tests and vouchers for glasses. For this reason it may be worth claiming Family Credit even if the weekly payments will be low. Family Credit is paid for 26 weeks, regardless of any changes in circumstances. If someone is thinking of claiming in March it might be worthwhile waiting until April, when the rates are adjusted. Similarly it is best to claim when income is at its lowest.

Housing Benefit; Social Fund

Families on a low income may also be eligible for **Housing Benefit** and help from the **Social Fund** (see sections 4.3 and 4.4).

WORDCHECK

passport benefit A social security benefit which gives automatic entitlement to another benefit.

This leaflet explains how some benefits take child care costs into account

EXAMPLE: FAMILY CREDIT

Mr and Mrs Ram have three children, aged 5, 7 and 13. Mrs Ram does not work and Mr Ram has a net income of £100 a week. The family has no savings. The maximum credit for the family is:

Adult credit	£46.45
Child aged 5	£11.75
Child aged 7	£11.75
Child aged 13	£19.45
	£89.40

Mr Ram's wages are more than the applicable amount of £75.20. The excess is £24.80 (£100.00 – £75.20). Seventy per cent of this difference (that is, 70 per cent of £24.80) is £17.36. The maximum Family Credit is therefore reduced by £17.36. The Family Credit payable is £72.04 (£89.40 – £17.36).

The family's total income will be made up of the wages, the Family Credit and the Child Benefit. They will also be entitled to free prescriptions, dental care, sight tests and glasses.

4.6 Benefits for people out of work

The Jobseeker's Allowance

In October 1996 a new benefit for unemployed people was introduced called the **Jobseeker's Allowance (JSA)**. This replaced two benefits for unemployed people: unemployment benefit and income support. To qualify for Jobseeker's Allowance, claimants must be over 18 and meet the following criteria:

- they must be working less than 16 hours a week;
- they must be available for work;
- they must have entered into a Jobseeker's Agreement;
- they must be actively seeking work;
- they must be capable of work;
- they must not be in full-time education;
- they must be resident in Great Britain.

(See section 6.1 for details of procedures relating to claiming JSA.)

There are two forms of Jobseeker's Allowance: Contributory Jobseeker's Allowance and Income-based Jobseeker's Allowance.

Contributory Jobseeker's Allowance

This is for people who have paid sufficient national insurance contributions. It lasts for six months only and there are no payments for dependents. (People with dependents have to claim income-based Jobseeker's Allowance as well.)

Income-based Jobseeker's Allowance

This is for people who have not paid enough contributions and whose income and savings are below set levels. It is paid in a similar way to Income Support with a personal allowance plus additions for dependent family members, premiums and mortgage interest payments. People whose partners work less than 24 hours per week can still claim but all earnings except for £10 a week will be deducted from the benefit. People receiving income-based Jobseeker's Allowance can claim Housing Benefit, Council Tax Benefit and other benefits which people on Income Support are entitled to.

People who work part-time will be allowed to keep:

- £5 a week in the case of a single, childless person;
- £10 a week for a couple;
- £15 a week for a single parent;
- £15 a week for a person with a disability.

The Back to Work Bonus

This is a bonus payment paid to people who have worked part-time while claiming Jobseeker's Allowance. It is paid when people get a full-time job and stop claiming. They are then entitled to receive half the earnings which have been deducted from the benefit paid. There is normally a limit of £1000 to the bonus payment.

Housing Benefit and the Social Fund

People who are unemployed and renting their home will be eligible for **Housing Benefit** to help with the rent (see section 4.4). They may also be able to get help from the **Social Fund** (see section 4.3).

Finding out more: the Jobseeker's Allowance

The Jobseeker's Allowance is a complicated benefit with many rules relating to such things as availability for work and what it means to be actively seeking work. For details of all the rules consult one of the books listed in the introduction to this chapter or ask at the JobCentre.

EXAMPLE 1: JOBSEEKER'S ALLOWANCE

Jaswinder has just finished studying at a university. She is 21 and not able to find work straightaway. She qualifies for Jobseeker's Allowance. She receives:

Eligibility

Personal allowance	£37.90	
Premiums: none	£ 0.00	
		→ £37.90

Deductions

None	£ 0.00	
		→ £ 0.00

Jobseeker's Allowance paid: £37.90

This money will have to cover everything except rent. The rent will be paid with Housing Benefit (section 4.4), assuming the level of rent is not too high.

EXAMPLE 2: JOBSEEKER'S ALLOWANCE

John is unemployed. He has been unemployed for two years. He has four children: Jim aged 14, Sally aged 10, and twins Sam and Jo aged 5. His wife Mary works part-time and earns £15. The applicable amounts for the family are:

Eligibility

Personal allowance:

John and Mary	£75.20
Jim	£24.10
Sally	£16.45
Sam	£16.45
Jo	£16.45

Premiums:

family	£10.55
	→ £159.20

The income to be counted is the Child Benefit and all except the first £10 of Mary's wages.

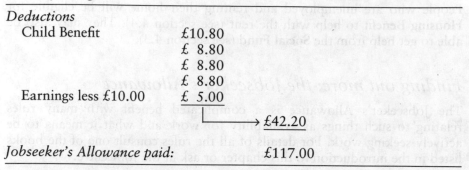

Deductions

Child Benefit	£10.80
	£ 8.80
	£ 8.80
	£ 8.80
Earnings less £10.00	£ 5.00
	→ £42.20

Jobseeker's Allowance paid: £117.00

The family's total income will be £169.20 (Jobseeker's Allowance, plus child benefit, plus earnings). In addition they may qualify for help with mortgage interest payments on a house they owner-occupy. (If they rent their home, they can claim Housing Benefit.)

4.7 Benefits for people who are sick or disabled

Incapacity

The first three benefits described here – Statutory Sick Pay, Incapacity Benefit and Severe Disablement Allowance – are paid to people who are unable to work because of illness or disability. Detailed rules set out exactly how this is decided. For the first 28 weeks people are entitled to benefit if they are incapable of doing their own job; after this the incapacity must be for any work. This is assessed objectively by deciding whether people can perform certain mental and physical functions which are set out in a list with points allocated to each ability. The exact rules concerning this test are very complicated. You or your client will need to get more information from an adviser or from a more detailed source (see the introduction to this chapter).

Statutory sick pay

When someone with a job is ill, the employer must pay sick pay. This is known as **statutory sick pay (SSP)**. SSP is paid at a rate of £54.55 a week. People who earn less than £61 do not pay national insurance contributions and are not eligible for SSP. Statutory sick pay is not paid for the first three days and lasts for 28 weeks.

Many employers are more generous than the law requires them to be and have their own occupational sick pay schemes. These often pay full wages for a limited period of time and then half wages for another period.

People who do not qualify for SSP should claim Incapacity Benefit (see below) and Income Support (see earlier in this chapter).

Incapacity Benefit

After entitlement to Statutory Sick Pay ends, people who are still incapable of work move on to Incapacity Benefit. People who are not eligible for SSP but who have been credited with contributions receive Incapacity Benefit from the beginning. In this case, it is paid at a lower rate. There are three rates of benefit. The short-term lower rate is paid for the first six months, followed by short-term higher rate. The long-term rate is paid after a year of claiming benefit.

Severe Disablement Allowance

This benefit is paid to people who have been incapable of work for six months and who are severely disabled or who are under 20. It is paid to people aged 16 to 65. There is a basic weekly allowance and an age-related addition.

Disability Living Allowance (DLA)

The **Disability Living Allowance** is a benefit introduced in 1992, replacing the Attendance Allowance and the Mobility Allowance. It has two parts: a care component and a mobility component.

Incapacity benefit was introduced in 1995 for people unable to work due to illness or disability

The care component

The care component is paid to people who are disabled and need attention from a carer. To qualify, people must need help with basic things such as washing and eating, or need supervision to avoid danger. There is an upper age limit of 65. (Older people who need help can claim the Attendance Allowance, which has two rates – a higher rate for those who need help by day *and* night, and a lower rate for those who need help in the day *or* the night.) To get the Disability Living Allowance, people must have been needing help for three months and be likely to need it for another six months. This qualifying period is waived in the case of people with terminal illnesses.

The care component is paid at three rates. The top rate is paid to people who need attendance by day *and* night. The middle rate is for those who need help by day *or* night. The lowest rate can be claimed by someone under 65 who needs help for part of the day or who cannot manage to cook a meal. The cooking test does not apply to a child under 16: a child will qualify if he or she needs more attention than other children of the same age.

No medical examination is needed to qualify for these benefits, and the payments are not affected by savings or other income.

The mobility component

The mobility component of the DLA is for people who have trouble getting about or who need to be accompanied outside. This includes people who cannot walk, those who are deaf and blind, and people with severe learning difficulties.

Claimants must be over 5. You cannot make a fresh claim if over the age of 65, but people who have been receiving the benefit from a younger age will continue to get it.

There are two rates for this part of the DLA: a higher and a lower rate, paid according to the extent to which a person's ability to get about is limited.

The higher rate of the mobility component of the DLA can be used to lease or buy a car from a charitable organisation called **Motability**. Under this scheme the benefit is paid direct to the charity.

The Disability Working Allowance (DWA)

The **Disability Working Allowance** is for people aged over 16 who work at least 16 hours a week. People must be 'disadvantaged' in getting a job by their disability. This includes physical and mental disabilities. The benefit is means-tested on the basis of savings and income. The same rules and levels of income apply as for other means-tested benefits, and the amount is calculated in a similar way to Family Credit. It is, however, paid to all people with disabilities, whether or not they have children. Like Family Credit, the benefit is paid for 26 weeks, regardless of any changes in circumstances. To qualify for the benefit the person must have been getting a disability benefit in the eight weeks before claiming DWA.

Disablement Benefit

There are different benefits for people who are injured at work or who have one of the designated industrial diseases. **Disablement Benefit** can be claimed by people 90 days after an industrial injury or the start of an industrial disease.

The amount paid depends on the degree of the disability. This is assessed in terms of percentages. As an indication, the loss of both hands is classed as 100 per cent, whereas the loss of a thumb counts as 30 per cent disablement.

Constant Attendance Allowance

There is also a **Constant Attendance Allowance**, which can be claimed on top of a 100 per cent Disablement Benefit by someone who needs constant attendance. There is a higher rate and a lower rate. The rate given depends on the degree of disability and the level of attendance required.

Income Support, Housing Benefit and the Social Fund

People with disabilities may receive **Income Support** (section 4.1), **Housing Benefit** (section 4.4) and help from the **Social Fund** (section 4.3). Income Support includes disability premiums which can be claimed by people receiving the Attendance Allowance.

Finding out more: benefits for people with disabilities

★ For further information on the Motability scheme, contact the organisation directly.

★ People with disabilities wanting information on benefits (and anything else concerned with disability) can contact DIAL (Disablement Information and Advice Lines). The local address should be in *The Phone Book*; the national address is given in the appendix.

★ For information on benefits for people with disabilities, see the *Disability Rights Handbook*. This is available from the Disability Alliance.

4.8 Help for people with disabilities

The Independent Living 93 Fund

The **Independent Living 93 Fund** was set up to help severely disabled people to live in the community. It can provide assistance for people who wish to leave a residential home or those who want to stay in their own homes. People must be between 16 and 66 to claim, and meet the following conditions:

- They must be receiving the highest care component of the Disability Living Allowance;
- They must be able to live in the community for at least six months;
- They must have a low income and savings of less than £8000;
- They must be assessed by the local authority as being at risk of needing residential care or capable of leaving residential care to live in the community;
- They must receive at least £200 worth of services a week from the local authority and be assessed as needing extra care up to £300 a week.

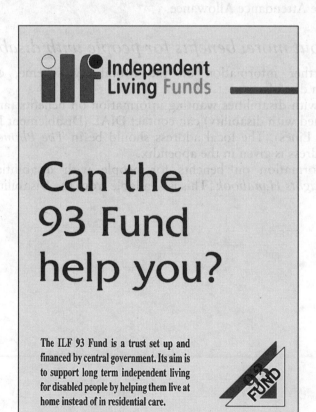

The Independent Living 93 Fund helps people with disabilities to live in the community

4.9 Help for families with a disabled child

The Family Fund

The **Family Fund** is financed by the government but run by an independent trust, the Joseph Rowntree Foundation in York. Payments are made to families which include a severely disabled child. The trust employs social workers who visit families to advise and to assess their needs.

Families are helped with things they would not otherwise be able to afford. The Fund does not provide for anything which could be obtained from another source, such as payments to do with education which could be claimed from the local education authority. The following are some examples of help given, taken from a leaflet prepared by the Family Fund:

- laundry equipment, for example a washing machine where a disability creates a lot of extra washing;
- holidays, for the whole family rather than just the child with a disability;
- outings, to provide relaxation for the family and stimulation for the child;
- driving lessons, for a parent;
- telephone installation and sometimes rental, if this is needed because of a child's medical condition;
- clothing and bedding, where a disability creates extra wear and tear;
- recreational items, if these are needed because of the disability.

The Family Fund can help families which include a child with a severe disability

4.10 Benefits for carers

Invalid Care Allowance

The **Invalid Care Allowance** is paid to people caring for someone who receives the Attendance Allowance, Constant Attendance Allowance or the higher or middle rates of the care component of the Disability Living Allowance. The carer need not be living with the person, but must be caring for him or her for 35 hours a week or more. The carer must be between the ages of 16 and 65, and not in work or full-time education.

As described in the introduction to this chapter, carers are entitled to **home responsibilities protection** which gives credits to their national insurance records.

4.11 Benefits for older people

Retirement pension

The rules about retirement pensions are quite complicated so just a basic outline will be given here.

To get a retirement pension there are two basic rules. First, people must be over retirement age. This is 60 for a woman and 65 for a man, but the age for women will be increased to 65 between the years 2010 and 2020. People must also meet the national insurance requirements. This means people must have paid national insurance contributions for most of their working life. In certain circumstances, national insurance contributions are credited – for example when someone stays at home to care for children or a person with a disability.

People may also be entitled to additional payments. There is an additional pension, paid under the **State Earnings-Related Pension Scheme** (**SERPS**). This is based on contributions since 1978 and the amount paid depends on the wages earned. Some people do not pay into this scheme – they are **contracted out** – because they have a different pension scheme, often through their work. These people receive the basic state pension plus an occupational or individual pension. An earlier scheme was the **graduated pension** scheme and some people receive extra money as a result of having paid into this when they were working between 1961 and 1975.

People over 80 have the princely sum of 25 pence a week added to their basic pension. People over 80 also qualify for a pension, even if they have not paid any contributions to national insurance.

Older people can continue working and still receive their retirement pension, but their pension will be taxed. They can, however, opt out of national insurance payments. It is also possible to defer pension payments for up to five years after retirement age and earn extra pension instead. The increase is about 7.5 per cent a year.

Income Support, Housing Benefit and the Social Fund

Older people also qualify for **Income Support** if their income falls below the level set for someone in their circumstances. There are premiums for older people, depending on age (see section 4.1). People may also qualify for Housing Benefit (section 4.4) if they rent a house or flat, and for help from the Social Fund (section 4.3).

Some older people will qualify for benefits awarded to people with disabilities (section 4.8).

Finding out more: benefits for older people

★ Age Concern produces free leaflets on benefits and pensions for older people.

★ Age Concern also produces an excellent book on benefits and other sources of finance for older people. This is called *Your Rights*. It is updated each year and is on sale in bookshops. It can also be bought directly from Age Concern.

benefits
ba
agency
An Executive Agency of the Department of Social Security

FB 6 From April 1996

Retiring?

Your pension and other benefits

Booklets from the Benefits Agency give clear explanations of entitlement to benefits

4.12 Benefits for widows

A woman whose husband has died qualifies for widows' benefits if he paid national insurance contributions.

Widows' Payment

For a **Widows' Payment** the husband must have paid national insurance for one year. The woman must be under 60 or else the husband must not have been eligible for a retirement pension at the time of his death. The payment is a one-off lump-sum.

Widowed Mothers' Allowance

The **Widowed Mothers' Allowance** is a weekly benefit paid to widows who are pregnant or who have children eligible for Child Benefit. The husband must have paid national insurance contributions for most of his working life.

Widows' Pension

A **Widow's Pension** is paid to widows aged between 45 and 65 at the time of their husband's death or at the time the Widowed Mothers' Allowance stopped. The benefit stops at age 65.

4.13 Benefits for women expecting a baby

Statutory Maternity Pay

Women in paid employment who become pregnant are entitled to **Statutory Maternity Pay (SMP)**. This is paid to all women who have worked with the same employer for at least 26 weeks and who are expecting a child in 11 weeks' time or who have recently had a baby. The higher rate of SMP is paid for the first six weeks – this is nine-tenths of the woman's average weekly wage. Then a lower rate is paid for seven weeks (although there are detailed rules about when the benefit can be claimed). Some employers have a more generous scheme for maternity pay, with longer periods and higher payments.

Maternity Allowance

Women who have recently given up their job or changed jobs can claim **Maternity Allowance**.

Maternity Expenses

Women on Income Support, income-based Jobseeker's Allowance or Family Credit can claim a **Maternity Expenses Grant** of £100 from the Social Fund.

4.14 Single parents – the Child Support Agency

The **Child Support Agency** (**CSA**) was set up in 1993 to operate a new system of child maintenance. The CSA assesses the financial situations of parents living apart to decide how much the 'absent parent' should pay for the children.

In deciding on the contribution of the 'absent parent' (the CSA's term for the parent who does not live with the children or who has fewer rights of care) the CSA looks at a number of factors. These include:

- the cost of maintaining a child;
- the income of each of the parents;
- any other children either parent might have.

There is a safeguard which means that no one should have to pay more than 30 per cent of their net income.

As well as assessment, the CSA can take on the role of collecting the payments from the absent parent and passing them to the 'parent with care'. The parent with care can ask for this service if he or she is worried that the absent parent will not pay.

Finding out more: the Child Support Agency

★   The Department of Social Security publishes booklets which provide a guide to the Child Support Agency.

★   For a comprehensive and detailed account of procedures and rules, the Child Poverty Action Group publishes and annually updates the *Child Support Handbook*.

The Child Support Agency decides how much parents living apart should contribute towards the maintenance of their children

4.16 Educational grants and loans

There are various types of grants available to students over the age of 16. **Mandatory awards** are paid by the local education authority. They include tuition fees and a means-tested grant towards living costs. Mandatory awards are given for full-time courses in universities or colleges which lead to degrees, Diplomas in Higher Education (DipHE), Higher National Diplomas (HND) and Post-Graduate Certificates in Education (PGCE). In most cases, acceptance onto one of these courses qualifies students for a grant.

Grants for full-time advanced courses are means-tested. For young people, an assessment will be made of the parents' income. This takes account of the number of people dependent on the income, and of some other costs such as mortgage interest payments. Parents' income is not looked at if the student is 'independent': there are several criteria for this. One is that the student must be aged over 25. Younger people are seen as being independent if they have supported themselves by a job for three years or for two or more periods adding up to three years. Others are seen as independent if they have been married for two years, or have been in care with the local authority for two years. The grant pays for fees and living costs.

STUDENT GRANTS AND LOANS

A BRIEF GUIDE FOR HIGHER EDUCATION STUDENTS 1996/97

D/EE
Department for Education and Employment

Grants and loans are available for students at university or a college of higher education

Local authorities can also offer **discretionary awards**. Policies on these awards vary from area to area. Discretionary awards may be made to individuals applying for a course which usually would qualify for a mandatory award but who are not themselves eligible, or for other courses, such as those leading to further education qualifications. Discretionary grants may only cover fees or may include a contribution towards living expenses. Local authorities can also provide funds for students with disabilities who attend colleges. Grants can cover the costs of special equipment such as computers or communication aids or pay for notetakers or interpreters.

Some types of qualification are funded from other authorities. For example, it is possible to train in occupational therapy, physiotherapy or dental hygiene with a grant from a health authority.

Students in higher education can apply for loans. Loans do not have to be paid back until the April after the end of the course (or after a student leaves a course). Interest does not have to be paid on the loan but the loan is indexed to the rate of inflation. This means the value of the amount paid back will be the same as the value of the amount borrowed. The government decides the rate of **indexation**, based on the rate of inflation. If, on leaving education, someone earns less than 85% of the national average earnings, they can put off repaying the loan for a year. This can be done each year that the person's income is lower than 85% of the average.

Career Development Loans are available to cover the fees of courses related to a job (see Chapter 6).

Colleges have **access funds** to help students with severe financial difficulties. There are limited amounts of money available in these funds and often a large number of students competing for help. Colleges decide their own policies on allocation of access funds.

WORDCHECK

mandatory award   A grant paid by the local education authority to all students on courses leading to particular qualifications.

access fund   A college fund to help students with severe financial difficulties.

means-tested benefit   A benefit awarded to some and not to others, according to the individual client's income and savings.

discretionary benefit   A benefit awarded to some and not to others, the decision being taken by an official according to the merits of the individual case.

Finding out more: educational grants and loans

★ Publications from the Department for Education and Employment (DfEE) include:

● *Student Grants and Loans: A Brief Guide for Higher Education Students*;
● *The Charter for Higher Education*;
● *The Charter for Further Education*.

TO FIND OUT

1 Contact the local education authority to find out the policy on paying fees and expenses for people studying at colleges of further education, but taking courses below degree level.

2 Contact the local college and find out what help they can offer to people on low incomes.

3 Find out what help is available for people with disabilities who want to study.

TO DO

Consider those of your clients who are in receipt of welfare benefits.

● Which benefits do they receive?
● Looking at the information in this chapter, which benefits are they entitled to?
● If there is a difference, what are the reasons for this? Could you, and if so should you, do anything about this difference?

TO DO

What benefits, if any, would the people in the following situations be entitled to?

(a) Judrani, a 16-year-old boy who has left school this month and is living with his family.

(b) Maggie, a single parent, not working, who is caring for two children at home.

(c) Mr Shang, a man who has just been made redundant after working for ten years.

(d) Kika, a woman who started work three months ago and has lost her job. Her husband earns £200 a week.

(e) Lindsay, a woman who gave up work to care for her elderly and disabled mother.

(f) The Wells family – the father works in a well-paid job and the mother has a part-time job. One of the three children is severely disabled and confined to a wheelchair.

(g) Robyn, a woman with three children under 16, whose husband has died.

(h) Peter, a man of 68 who has had a lifelong disability and has never worked.

(i) Jill, a woman who changed jobs, then found she was pregnant.

(j) Mike, a man with a learning disability who is moving from a hospital into the community.

5 Daily living

Our world is becoming increasingly competitive and fast-moving. People are expected to be able to look after themselves and to get ahead. It seems that people have less time for, and show less patience towards, those whose physical or learning disability means they cannot move at the world's pace. At the same time, there is a move away from the idea that people should live apart from society, in residential institutions. The current thinking is that, as far as possible, people with physical or learning disabilities should live at home in the local community.

This chapter is about the services and facilities which aim to enable people with disabilities and other special needs to live full and independent lives. If you are involved in providing care you need to know something of the range of services available. Some services are provided by private and voluntary organisations; others are provided within the social services department or by the health authority. The task of care workers is to co-ordinate services into a complete **package of care** which meets the needs of the individual person. At the time of writing (1996) it is expected that local authorities will soon be able to give people the money with which to purchase services for themselves, although they do not presently have this power.

Note that references to disability in the legislation include physical disabilities, learning disabilities and people suffering from mental illnesses.

The 1990 NHS and Community Care Act

The 1990 NHS and Community Care Act provides the framework for the organisation of care. The Act requires local authorities to prepare community care plans for their areas in consultation with other organisations such as health-care providers.

Local authorities are also required to carry out an assessment of individuals needing social care and support. The authority must make available the criteria for entitlement to an assessment. The assessment will cover all aspects of a person's life including:

- biographical details;
- physical health;
- mental health;
- race and culture;
- the needs of any carers;
- social network and support;
- the client's own perception of his or her needs.

Assessments are carried out by various professionals including social workers, occupational therapists and community psychiatric nurses. Clients and carers should be involved in the assessment and their own feelings taken into account. The client's ability to pay for services will also be assessed along with their need for services.

Following the assessment, the local authority will decide which needs are to be met. A **care plan** will then be prepared showing how the needs are to be met. Where people have complex needs, they will be allocated a **care manager** to arrange and oversee the care plan.

The legislation encourages the local authority to use the **independent sector** to provide services – this includes voluntary organisations and private companies. The local authority's role is to purchase services on behalf of clients and to monitor provision.

Local authorities can charge for services but must make services available to people who cannot afford to pay. The charges vary from area to area.

Legislation on disability

Earlier legislation which is still relevant to people with a disability includes The Chronically Sick and Disabled Persons Act 1970. Under this Act, local authorities must arrange provision which is necessary to meet the needs of people with a disability. The services which must be provided are:

- help in the home;
- home-loan equipment;
- meals;
- a telephone;
- help with joining in education or leisure activities;
- holidays.

The Disabled Persons (Services, Consultation and Representation) Act 1986 extended the rights of people with disabilities to assessment, information and advocacy. These rights are now included in the NHS and Community Care Act.

Finding out more: community care

★ *The Community Care Handbook* (second edition, 1995) by Barbara Meredith is an excellent detailed and practical guide to community care. It is published by Age Concern England.

★ Age Concern produces a factsheet called *Disability and Ageing: Your Rights to Social Services*, which is written specifically for older people with a disability but which is also relevant in some other situations.

★ *Oi! It's My Assessment* is a guide to community care produced by People First, for people with learning disabilities.

TO DO

1 Obtain a copy of the local authority's plan for community care in your area.

2 Find out the criteria for entitlement to an assessment.

3 Find out the policy of the local authority on charging for services.

TO DO

1 Survey your local area to see how accessible it is for people confined to wheelchairs. Check widths of doorways, numbers of steps, availability of lifts, and access to toilets.

2 If possible, borrow a wheelchair and work with a colleague, finding out what it is like to negotiate a town or village with a wheelchair. Set yourself a number of tasks, such as buying a stamp, using a phone, going to the toilet, having a drink, or getting a bus.

As an alternative, you could try the same tasks with a pram. Using a pram will not give you the same insight into the psychological difficulties of being in a wheelchair, but some of the practical problems are similar.

3 Find out whether there is a guide written for people with disabilities trying to use facilities in your area. If not, you could consider writing one. Local schools, colleges or voluntary organisations may be prepared to help. Local businesses might help with the costs of printing and distribution.

5.1 Getting about

Access

The 1970 Chronically Sick and Disabled Persons Act made it a duty for designers and owners of new buildings to consider the needs of people with disabilities. A further development came in 1981. The Disabled Persons Act of that year gave planning authorities the duty of drawing people's attention to provisions relating to access. This must be done when planning permission is granted.

These provisions were extended in 1985. Certain new buildings must now provide access and facilities for people with disabilities. These include offices, shops, single-storey factories, educational buildings and others which admit the public. Local authorities have begun to employ **access officers** to oversee these regulations.

Finding out more: access for disabled people

★ For further information on the legislation and regulations concerning access to buildings, contact the Disabled Living Foundation.

★ There are local guides to a number of towns and cities, written for people with disabilities. These are produced locally, but under the umbrella of the Royal Association for Disability and Rehabilitation (RADAR). These guides give details of public buildings, including information on door widths, the number of steps in the building, and the toilet facilities. A list of the booklets available can be obtained from RADAR.

Mobility aids

Walking aids such as walking sticks, crutches and Zimmer frames can be borrowed from the health authority or from voluntary organisations such as the Red Cross. Wheelchairs are also available for loan. *Motability*

Access officers check that new buildings meet the requirements for people with disabilities

Disabled Living Foundation

The Disabled Living Foundation provides information for people with disabilities

Mobility aids – walking frames and wheelchairs

Walking frames:

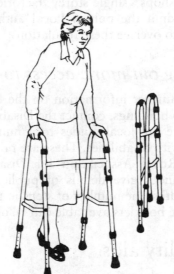

folding frame

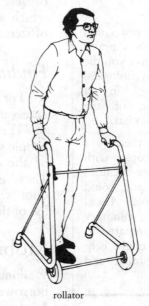

rollator

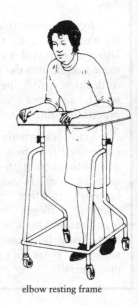

elbow resting frame

Pushed wheelchair

Power driven wheelchair

Batricar

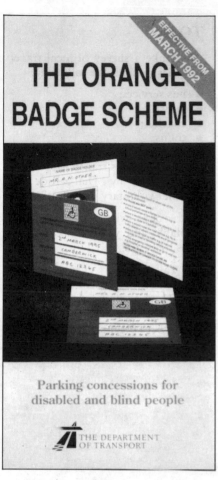

The Orange Badge scheme allows people with disabilities to park nearer to where they are going

provides a hire-purchase scheme for people receiving the Mobility component of the Disability Living Allowance to enable them to buy electric wheelchairs.

Motability can also help with the purchase of single-person electric vehicles for people with disabilities. (See Chapter 4 for details about the Disability Living Allowance and how to use this to lease a car through Motability.)

Parking

The **Orange Badge scheme** is a national system of parking concessions for people with disabilities. It includes disabled people who are travelling as drivers or as passengers, including those who are blind. The scheme allows people to park nearer to where they are going by waiving some of the rules which apply to others.

People are entitled to an Orange Badge if they receive the Mobility component of the Disability Living Allowance, or are blind, or have a permanent and substantial disability which makes walking impossible or very difficult. Badges are issued by the local social services department.

Finding out more: the Orange Badge scheme

★ A leaflet is available giving details of the Orange Badge scheme. It is published by the Department of Transport and is available from social services or from the Department of Transport Mobility Unit.

Public transport

Most areas have concessionary bus-fare schemes for older people. These are of various types and may mean free bus travel at off-peak times or reduced fares.

In Greater London there is a **Taxicard** system for people with disabilities. The card entitles people to reduced fares.

British Rail offer a **Disabled Person's Railcard** which gives discounts of 50 per cent for a disabled person and a companion. The **Senior Railcard** gives discounts to people over 60. Leaflets are available from local stations which give details of these schemes. British Rail also produces a leaflet which gives details for people with disabilities of the facilities available at various stations. RADAR also produces a guide to travel on trains for people with disabilities.

For travel by air there are leaflets detailing the special support services available at various airports.

Special services

Dial-a-Ride is a door-to-door transport system for people with disabilities who are unable to use public transport. Bookings are made in advance, by telephone. A number of voluntary organisations offer the service of volunteer drivers using their own cars. In some cases these are free, in others a small charge is made. The WRVS provides a shopping service with specially adapted minibuses. In some cases the health authority and the social services provide transport. Again, there may be a charge. Information on these services is available from the Community Transport Association.

Going nowhere fast

Finding out more: transport

★ The Community Transport Association (CTA) provides advice and information on accessible voluntary and community transport, publishes leaflets and a magazine and provides training.

★ Information on public transport in London is available from the London Regional Transport Unit for Disabled Passengers.

★ Advice to drivers with disabilities is provided by the Mobility Advice and Vehicle Information Service (MAVIS) and the Mobility Information Service (MIS).

★ DaRT Dial-A-Ride and Taxicard Users provide information on these schemes.

★ Age Concern produces factsheets on travel for older people.

★ RADAR has information on all aspects of disability, including mobility and transport. It publishes a number of booklets on travel arrangements. Write to the address in the appendix for a list of publications.

★ The British Airports Authority (BAA) produces a special needs edition of its guide to Heathrow Airport called *Travellers' Information*.

★ *Flying High* is a guide to air travel for older people and people with disabilities produced by the Disabled Living Foundation.

TO DO

1 Make a survey of local travel facilities. Include the following:

- bus services;
- taxis;
- coaches;
- trains;
- the underground (if applicable);
- social services transport;
- transport by Dial-a-Ride or other voluntary organisations.

Find out what facilities are available and what concessionary fares there are.

2 Talk to clients with disabilities. What services do they use? How well are these services tailored to their needs? How could the services be improved?

DaRTabout

the independent voice of dial-a-ride & taxicard users

DaRT
No. 8 Spring 1996

Dial-a-Ride

Taxicard

Public transport

SPECIAL ANNUAL REPORT ISSUE

Dial-a-Ride offers a door-to-door transport system for people with disabilities

5.2 Leisure

There are a number of services and organisations working to help people with disabilities to participate in leisure activities.

Books, radios and televisions

Most local authorities provide a **travelling library** service which brings library books to people's homes. Social services may be able to provide radios and televisions for people with disabilities. An organisation called *British Wireless for the Blind Fund* will lend radios free of charge to blind people. For those who are housebound, there is *Wireless for the Bedridden*, which loans radios and televisions. For people with a visual impairment the Royal National Institute for the Blind (RNIB) lends books in Braille and Moon type and provides a Talking Book Service.

Sports and leisure

Many sports centres have facilities for people with disabilities. The RADAR guides to local areas (referred to above, under 'Access') provide information on the accessibility of sports facilities as well as other services. There are also many specialist organisations offering information and special provision for people with disabilities. Some examples are listed below. The Disabled Living Foundation can provide up-to-date information on services available.

Finding out more: sports and leisure

★ The British Sports Association for Disabled People can provide details of sports clubs. Organisations catering for particular disabilities, such as the RNIB, also provide information and support for leisure and sports activities.
★ Horticultural Therapy provides information on gardening equipment.

Holidays

Various organisations can provide information on holidays for disabled people and their carers. It may be possible to get financial help towards a holiday from social services or from a charitable organisation. Organisations for specific illnesses and conditions, such as the Kidney Patients Association, may have special arrangements to help people with holidays.

PHAB (Physically Handicapped and Able-Bodied) is an organisation which tries to break down barriers and stereotypes by bringing people with disabilities and able-bodied people together. The organisation consists of local groups which arrange social clubs, outings and holidays.

The Holiday Care Service is a national charity which provides holiday information and support for people with disabilities and others, including single parents. The Holiday Care Service also provides discount booking services.

The Holiday Care Service provides holiday information and discounts on holidays

Finding out more: holidays

★ Age Concern produces a factsheet on holidays for older people.
★ MENCAP publishes an annual holiday accommodation guide.
★ RADAR publishes guides to holidays in the British Isles and abroad and also *Holiday Fact Packs* covering general information, transport and equipment and specialised accommodation.

TO DO

One of the problems for people with disabilities in using leisure facilities is that of access. Survey the recreational facilities in your area from the point of view of a person in a wheelchair. Look at:

● cinemas;
● bingo halls;
● theatres;
● discos;
● nightclubs;
● sports centres;
● swimming pools;
● pubs.

5.3 Care and support

The majority of people who are older or who have a disability live in their own homes. They may need help with domestic or personal tasks. This section looks at the services available to help. The section also looks at facilities providing care, on a non-residential basis, in day centres; and at an innovatory system of care in another person's home.

The section at the beginning of this chapter described how care and support is arranged according to the provisions of the NHS and Community Act, with an assessment and a care plan, monitored in more complex situations by a care manager.

Social services departments

The local social services department is usually the starting point for these kinds of services. Social workers or other staff within the department will assess the needs of the individual and any carers. A range of services may be co-ordinated to provide a care plan which will be monitored and reviewed from time to time. Social workers also provide advice, information and counselling for clients and their carers. They will also liaise with voluntary and other organisations who may help to provide care and support.

Help at home

The tasks carried out by home-care staff vary according to the policies and priorities of the local authority but may include housework, bathing, shopping, help with dressing and going to bed. In some cases, live-in help may be provided. The services may be free, charged at a flat rate, or vary according to the income and savings of the client.

It is now common for home-care staff not to be employed by the local authority but to be contracted from a private or voluntary organisation. People can also pay privately for these services. As mentioned at the beginning of this chapter it is anticipated that local authorities will be given the power to give people money to purchase services from a provider of their choice. Currently (1996) this is not the case.

Relief for carers

Crossroads Care Attendance Scheme is a national voluntary organisation funded jointly by health authorities and social services. It provides relief for carers of people with disabilities by helping with practical tasks. Care attendants are trained and employed to take over the role of the carer and to give a break when this is most needed.

Meals

The **meals-on-wheels** service (sometimes called community meals) delivers hot meals at midday to older people and others living in the community. The service is usually administered by the social services department but run by a voluntary organisation such as the WRVS. There is a charge for the meals, but this is usually less than the cost. Referrals are through doctors and social workers. Social services assess clients to see whether they qualify for the service.

Incontinence

For people who have problems with incontinence, there are laundry schemes. These may be attached to the home-help service or run by the health authority. Laundry is collected and delivered. The health authority may also supply various items such as commodes and incontinence pads. Some areas employ a **continence nurse adviser** to provide counselling, advice and information.

Day care

There are various types of **day centres**, provided by social services, the health authority and voluntary organisations. Older people may attend day centres attached to residential homes. These would allow a carer to work in the day or simply to have a break. Organisations such as Age Concern run centres providing recreational activities and usually a midday meal.

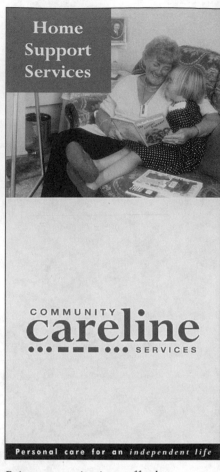

Private organisations offer home care services for people with disabilities

Some areas have innovative schemes for day care

There are also day centres which concentrate on teaching living skills to help people with physical or learning disabilities.

Some areas have innovative schemes, such as *Homeshare Daycare* which runs in Ipswich. This provides day care for elderly people in family homes. The scheme employs experienced people who each take a small number of elderly people into their homes on a daily basis. Transport is provided. This scheme works as an alternative to day care in residential homes and day centres.

A different scheme for children with learning disabilities is **shared care**. Here carers are recruited to care for children for up to 20 days a year. This gives the parents a break, as well as providing wider experiences for the child.

Finding out more: help at home

★ Age Concern produces a useful factsheet called *Finding Help at Home*. It is available from the Information and Policy Department of Age Concern England.

★ See also the sources listed in the introduction to this chapter and in section 5.5.

TO THINK ABOUT

There have been various changes in the way in which services are provided and delivered. A new proposal is that people could be given money and could themselves employ the help they need, instead of being given services by the local authority.

Is this a good idea? What would be the advantages and disadvantages of this form of service delivery? What are the views of your colleagues and your clients?

TO DO

Find out what help is available locally for those living at home.

1 Who runs the meals-on-wheels service? Is it available every day? What are the prices? Does the service cater to the needs of people from ethnic minorities and others with special dietary needs?

2 Does the social services department charge for home helps? How much? Is there a private service operating in the area?

3 Do any voluntary organisations provide home-care services? Is the Crossroads scheme available?

4 Are there any initiatives in providing day care in people's own houses? What sort of day centres are provided? Is there provision for older people, for people with physical or learning disabilities, and for people with mental illnesses?

TO DO

Interview some people about the services they receive.

- Are they happy with the services that are available?
- Would they like more support? Would they prefer support of a different type?

5.4 Equipment to help with daily living

Occupational therapists are employed by social services and by health authorities. Their work is concerned with helping people with disabilities to live as independently as possible. They visit people at home to assess their situation and needs. They can teach people alternative approaches to tasks and problems. They also advise people on special equipment which will make things easier.

There is a vast range of special equipment designed for people with disabilities. Equipment exists for most personal and domestic tasks. Some examples are mechanical chairs to help people stand from sitting; special cutlery and plates for those who have problems with hand movements; and equipment to make bathing or showering safer and easier. Equipment can be borrowed from the local authority or the health service, or bought. Equipment such as that shown below for helping people in bed is most likely to be available through the health service.

There is a vast range of special equipment for people with disabilities

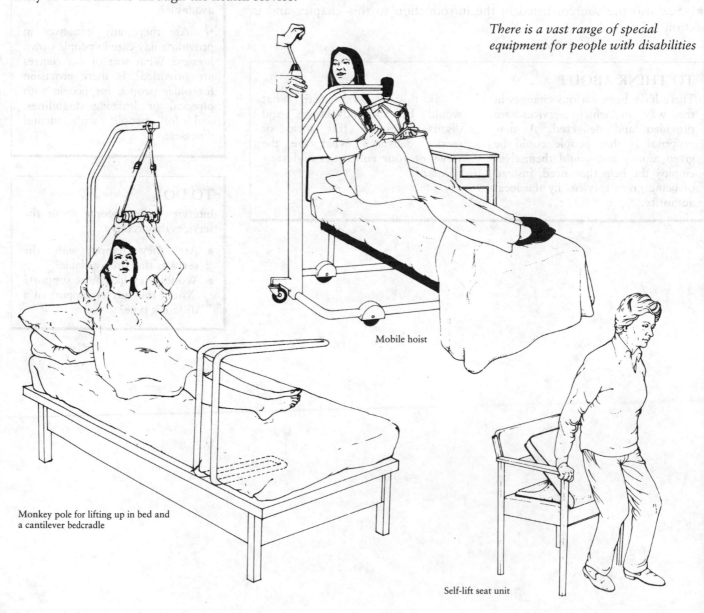

Mobile hoist

Monkey pole for lifting up in bed and a cantilever bedcradle

Self-lift seat unit

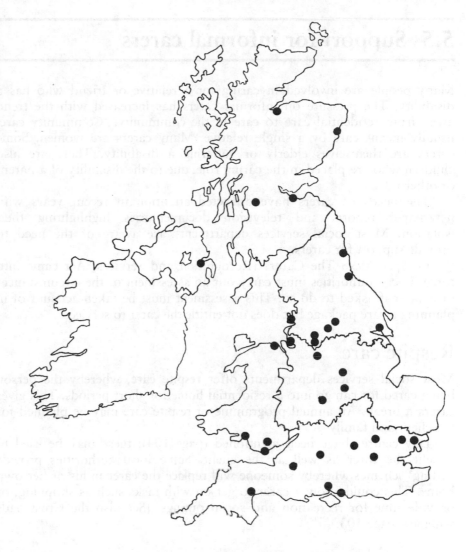

Locations of disabled living centres

Trying out special equipment

Some areas have **Disabled Living Centres**. These centres stock a range of special equipment. They can be visited by people with disabilities and their carers; equipment is demonstrated and can be tried out. Occupational therapists are on hand to give advice and information. The centres may be run by voluntary organisations, by the health service or by social services. There is also a travelling exhibition which tours Scotland.

Finance

Grants are available from social services to pay for major adaptations to homes such as putting in a lift. The family will be expected to contribute to the cost, depending on its income.

Finding out more: home-loan equipment

★ The Disabled Living Foundation provides information on equipment as well as on other aspects of disability. It offers a number of useful publications, including the leaflet *Aids and Equipment for People with Disabilities*.

5.5 Support for informal carers

Many people are involved in caring for a relative or friend who has a disability. The pressure on informal carers has increased with the trend away from residential care to care in the community. 'Community care' usually means care by a single relative. Many carers are women. Some carers are themselves elderly or suffering a disability. There are also children who are placed in the caring role, due to the disability of a parent or other relative.

The needs of carers have attracted attention in recent years with newspaper reports and television documentaries highlighting their isolation. Most social services departments are aware of the need to provide support for carers.

In April 1996 The Carers (Recognition and Services) Act came into force. Local authorities must carry out an assessment of the circumstances of a carer if asked to do so. This assessment must be taken account of in planning a care package but does not entitle the carer to services.

Respite care

Most social services departments offer **respite care,** whereby the person being cared for can go into a residential home for short periods. This gives carers a break. An annual programme of respite care may be planned for the client and family.

Day centres have been mentioned (page 104): these may be used to benefit the carer as well as the client. Some local authorities provide **'sitting' schemes** whereby someone will replace the carer in his or her own home. This could allow a carer to get on with tasks such as shopping, or provide time for recreation and social outings. (See also the Crossroads scheme – page 103.)

Mutual support

The Carers National Association (*Carers*) was formed in 1988 as a result of merging two existing organisations for carers. This organisation provides advice and information with excellent leaflets on various aspects of caring and a bi-monthly journal. There are also local groups which provide support and other services. The Carers National Association also acts as a pressure group, bringing the needs of carers to the attention of the government and other policy-making bodies.

Young carers

There has been recent concern about children and young people who are caring for relatives at home. Carers National Association have a magazine for young carers called *Link* and a *Young Carers Information Pack*. These are free to young carers. Around the country there are a number of schemes run by local authorities or voluntary organisations to support young carers.

Carers provides support for people caring for a relative or friend

CASE STUDIES

Imagine that the following people are your clients. What help and advice would you offer them?

(a) Carol is 50. She cares for her mother, who lives with her. Her mother's physical and mental health is deteriorating. Carol is very reluctant to allow her mother to go into a residential home, but is concerned that she herself cannot cope.

(b) Nick and Jackie have a child with cerebral palsy. Although they have little money to spare, they are desperate to take their three children on holiday.

(c) Allen is 20. As a result of a childhood accident, he uses a wheelchair. He wants to go abroad alone, to visit relatives in America. He needs to find out about travel arrangements.

(d) Ivy is 78. She is crippled with arthritis and is finding it difficult to carry out many of the household tasks. Even small things like turning off the cooker taps present a problem.

Finding out more: support for carers

★ Leaflets and factsheets on all aspects of caring can be obtained from Carers National Association (the address is in the appendix).

★ *What to Do and Who to Turn To* is written by Marina Lewycka and published by Age Concern. It is written as a guide for someone starting to care for an elderly relative.

★ *Caring at Home* is written by Nancy Lohner and published by the King's Fund Centre.

WORDCHECK

assessment The procedure where a person's needs are defined and decisions made about the provision of services.

care manager The person who carries out the assessment, preparation of the care plan, organisation of services and monitoring and review.

independent sector Private and voluntary organisations providing welfare services.

voluntary organisation An organisation which has not been set up by a government body and which does not aim to make a profit.

access officers Employees of the local authority, who ensure that public buildings meet the requirements of access for people with disabilities.

home-care service A service which provides personal care, such as help with washing and dressing, in a client's own home.

continence nurse adviser Someone who provides counselling, advice and information for people with problems related to incontinence.

occupational therapist Someone who helps people with disabilities to live a normal life, teaching necessary skills and providing special equipment.

Disabled Living Centre A place where equipment available to help people with disabilities is demonstrated.

respite care Short-term care in a residential home for someone who is otherwise living with relatives or alone in the community.

6 Employment

Unemployment continues to be a serious problem in Britain. Some two million people are currently included in the official statistics, and even this high figure may not represent the true number of unemployed people. The government figure counts only people who are registered as out of work and eligible for benefit. This excludes certain people. One group to be excluded are young people who cannot claim benefits until they are 18. Another excluded group are the women who cannot claim benefit because of their husbands' income. It may well be that the real number of unemployed people is closer to three million.

Unemployment does not hit everyone in the population equally. Like most other things, it is unequally distributed amongst people. The groups of people who are more vulnerable include younger people, who will not be taken on in times of recession, and older people, who find it hard to get new jobs if they are made redundant. Members of ethnic minorities experience discrimination and find it harder to find and keep jobs than do white people. Adults with learning disabilities may find themselves at the bottom of the pile when there is not enough work to go around. Similarly, anyone with a less than totally respectable history – such as someone who has been in prison or someone who has spent time in a psychiatric hospital – may be rejected as a matter of course when there are 20 applicants for each job. These people, who may also be the clients of care workers, may need extra advice and help from you in looking for work.

The importance of employment

Helping someone to find a good job can prevent a lot of other problems. Work is very important in our society. Most obviously, it provides an income. Although there are benefits which can be claimed by people without work (see Chapter 4), these are very low and do not provide a very good standard of living. Most people in work are financially better off than people living on benefits.

The benefits of work are not only financial, however. Work provides a structure to the day. Days of unemployment are long and slow; people become bored, restless and depressed. Work provides company. For many people, work is the main source of friends. Unemployment is often very lonely. More than all of this, work can provide a sense of purpose and meaning. It gives status – a sense of *being* someone. This can be seen by the way people's first question on meeting a stranger is often 'What do you do?'

People who are unemployed are more likely to be in poor physical and mental health. Suicides are more common amongst unemployed people. A young person who can find a satisfying job may be prevented from getting into trouble with the police and courts. Adults with learning disabilities are likely to benefit from the opportunity to show what they can do, and from the sense of being part of society that work can give them.

TO DO
Survey the local employment opportunities.

- Look in the newspapers at the kinds of work being advertised.
- Visit the JobCentre. What sorts of jobs are available?
- Are there jobs for people without qualifications? Are there any jobs suitable for adults with learning disabilities? What sorts of rates of pay are being offered?

6.1 Advice and information

Finding out about vacancies

The best starting point for someone looking for work is the local JobCentre. Their address can be found in *The Phone Book* under 'Employment Service' or 'JobCentre'. Anyone can use the JobC112
entre. Job vacancies are displayed on cards. If a suitable vacancy is found, the staff will arrange an interview with the employer.

JobCentres also offer a wide range of information and advice and can provide the route into programmes aimed at helping people find work. Nearly all JobCentres offer a one-stop service for job-finding and benefit enquiries.

Vacancies are also advertised in local and national newspapers, depending on the type of job. Libraries hold copies of newspapers which can be viewed free of charge. Specialised journals advertise jobs in particular fields of work, for example the *Nursing Times* is a source of nursing jobs and *Community Care* advertises jobs in social work. Social work and related vacancies are advertised in *The Guardian* each Wednesday. There are also private employment agencies; some of these specialise in a particular type of work while others are more general.

Looking for work

When someone first signs on as unemployed at the JobCentre an appointment is made for a **'new jobseeker interview'**. This interview lasts about 30 minutes and is with an **Employment Officer**. Part of the purpose of the interview is to draw up a **jobseeker's agreement**.

Jobseeker's agreement

A jobseeker's agreement includes information about the type of work the person is looking for together with details such as the hours they are prepared to work and how far they can travel to work. It also includes a list of the steps the person is taking to look for work. This information is based on a questionnaire filled in by the claimant before the interview. The various points have to be agreed by the Employment Officer. The jobseeker's agreement is signed and a copy given to the claimant. When the jobseeker's agreement is first completed, people are usually allowed to include restrictions on such things as the level of pay they are prepared to work for. Later on, people are expected to take work whatever the pay (see below).

Fortnightly interviews

Most people attend the JobCentre once a fortnight to sign that they are still available for work. At the time of each visit, there is a short interview with the Employment Officer to check on the steps being taken to find work.

Thirteen-week advisory interviews

Someone who has been unemployed for 13 weeks will be asked to attend a full advisory interview. Here the Employment Officer will review the person's situation. If the person was allowed to restrict the jobs they were applying for, they will be told that they must now look at a broader range of work and not restrict the level of pay unreasonably. If the Employment Officer thinks the person is not doing enough to find work, he/she can issue a **jobseeker's direction** or refer the claim to an **Adjudication Officer** to decide if the person is still entitled to benefits. A job may be offered at the interview or the opportunity to participate in the following two voluntary employment schemes.

Travel to interview scheme

This scheme pays the cost of travelling to a job interview which is beyond the person's normal travelling distance from home. The job must be full-time and permanent to qualify.

Job search plus

This is a programme which lasts for three days and which is concerned with improving job-seeking skills. The aim is to decide on goals and work out how to achieve these goals. People are given help with writing a CV and preparing for interviews. There is also help in dealing with the experience of being turned down for jobs. At the end of the programme the person takes away an **Action Plan** which can be built on in later interviews with Employment Officers.

Six-monthly restart interviews

When someone has been unemployed for six months they will be asked to attend a **restart interview**. This has a similar purpose to the 13 week interview and again involves a review of the situation. However the person will also be told that they are now not allowed to place any restrictions on the level of pay they are prepared to work for. People will be informed of four more voluntary schemes which they are now eligible to attend.

Job interview guarantee scheme

This scheme is for people who have the right skills and qualifications for a job but who are finding difficulty in getting an interview – perhaps because of the length of time they have been unemployed, or because of a disability, or maybe a criminal record. People are guaranteed an interview with an employer. They may be asked to go on a five-day course to prepare themselves for the interview. The course will involve assessing the person's strengths and weaknesses.

Jobclub

This scheme lasts for four and half days a week for between 20 and 26 weeks. It involves an intensive search for work. The scheme helps people apply for jobs by providing telephones, newspapers, stationery and stamps. Fares are paid for people to attend Jobclub. There are specialist Jobclubs for people with particular special needs and for people looking for executive and managerial jobs.

Work trials

This scheme allows someone to work for up to 15 days without coming off benefit. In addition to their normal benefit, people receive expenses of up to £1.50 a day for meals and travel expenses of up to £10 a day.

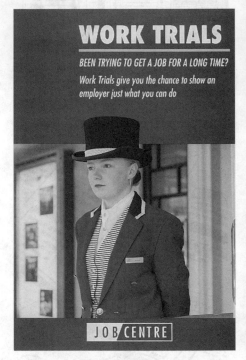

Work trials allow people to try a job for three weeks without losing benefit

Jobclubs offer free access to stationery, telephones, stamps and newspapers

Training for work

This programme provides training in new skills. People receive a training allowance of £10 a week in addition to their normal benefit.

Restart interviews after one year

People who continue to be unemployed receive interviews every six months. The interviews are similar, but different schemes become available as time goes on. Some of the schemes are compulsory and people will lose their benefit if they do not attend. After one year, people are entitled to attend any of the schemes described above, plus three additional ones.

Jobplan

This is a workshop which lasts for four and a half days in the first week, followed by a half-day session about two weeks later. The aim is to build up confidence through reviews with the workshop leaders. People can also work in small groups with others in similar positions and visit other programmes. This scheme is compulsory for people who do not take up an offer of employment or attend another course.

Workwise

This is a four-week programme for people aged 18–24. It is similar in its aims to Jobplan. Daily tasks are set to improve job-seeking skills and people complete an activity log. At the end the person will have developed an Action Plan which will be discussed with an Employment Officer to update their jobseeker's agreement. Like Jobplan, Workwise is compulsory. People will lose some entitlement to benefit if they do not attend or leave early.

1-2-1

This involves a series of six interviews with a senior Employment Officer. Attendance is compulsory. In the interviews the Employment Officer will look at the unemployed person's situation to see what is stopping the person from getting a job.

After 18 months

The only new programme at this stage is a **restart course**. People can attend one of these courses if they ask and there is a place available.

Restart course

A restart course lasts for two weeks and like the other courses tries to help people look for work. People attend in the morning and spend the afternoon completing tasks suggested by the course leader.

After two years

At this stage an unemployed person is required to attend a restart course and will lose benefits if he/she fails to attend. An employer giving someone a job who has been unemployed for two years does not have to pay national insurance for the first two weeks. Two other schemes available at this point are Jobfinder's grant and Jobmatch.

Jobfinder's grant

Under this scheme, someone can be paid a grant to take a job they would not have otherwise considered. The grant is to offset some of the costs of returning to work. The amount paid is usually £200.

Jobmatch
At the time of writing (1996), this is a pilot scheme running in some areas of the country. It allows people to take a part-time job of between 16 and 30 hours a week and receive an allowance of £50 a week. The allowance continues for six months, even if the job becomes full-time. There are two bonus payments for people who are still in work after the six month period. The payments are £50 and paid after six and twelve weeks.

WORDCHECK

Employment Officer   When people claim Jobseeker's Allowance, they are advised and monitored by an Employment Officer at the JobCentre.

jobseeker's agreement   This is a document completed when someone claims Jobseeker's Allowance. It includes details of how the claimant will look for work.

travel to interview scheme   This pays the cost of travel to an interview beyond the normal travelling distance of a person who has been out of work for 13 weeks or more.

job search plus   A scheme available to people who have been unemployed for 13 weeks which lasts for three days. The aim is to improve job-seeking skills.

restart interview   For people who have been out of work for six months. Review of Jobseeker's Agreement during an interview with an Employment Officer.

job interview guarantee scheme   Guarantees an interview for someone with the right skills and qualifications for a job.

Jobclub   A scheme which lasts for 20–26 weeks and involves an intensive search for work.

work trials   An opportunity to work for 15 days without coming off benefit. Expenses are paid.

training for work   Programme of training for unemployed people. Pays benefit plus £10.

Jobplan   A workshop for long-term unemployed people to improve their confidence.

Workwise   A four-week programme for younger unemployed people.

1-2-1   A series of six interviews with a senior Employment Officer.

restart course   A two-week course to help long-term unemployed people look for work.

jobfinder's grant   A grant paid to long-term unemployed people to offset the costs of returning to work.

Jobmatch   A scheme which pays a bonus to unemployed people taking part-time jobs.

Just the Job *describes the programmes and services aimed at getting people back to work. It is available from JobCentres*

Finding out more: looking for work

★ The Employment Service publishes a booklet describing the programmes and service aimed at helping unemployed people get back to work. Called *Just the Job* (reference JTJ1), it is available in all JobCentres and Employment Service offices.

★ As well as *Just the Job*, there are other booklets for people looking for work. One is *The Job Kit*, which covers applying for jobs, preparation of CVs and interview technique. It is also available from all JobCentres.

★ Age Concern publishes a book called *Changing Direction* which describes employment options in mid-life.

6.2 The Careers Service

Local authorities must provide careers advice for all young people at school. Careers officers visit schools, offering careers guidance and making young people aware of opportunities for employment and training. The local careers office also acts as an employment agency for young people aged between 16 and 18. It has training schemes on offer and liaises with local employers to keep tabs on the local job market.

The Careers Service has no statutory obligation to older people – no legislation requires that it provide a service for adults. However, most areas offer some form of adult guidance service. Anyone can contact this service for advice and information and to arrange a careers interview.

Colleges and universities also have their own careers advisers. Some colleges have Adult Guidance Centres which offer a range of information and advice on careers, education and training. There are charters for further and higher education which set out students' rights to information as well as to education. Also individual institutions have their own charters.

All the careers services can provide access to computer programmes designed to help people match their interests and abilities with jobs and to find out about the training required for particular jobs.

6.3 Training and educational opportunities

Training and Enterprise Councils (TECs) in England and **Local Enterprise Companies (LECs)** in Scotland are responsible to the Department of Employment for government-financed training schemes. They are led by local business people and aim to meet local training needs with flexible provision. They provide a number of different services.

Training and work experience

TECs are responsible for programmes of training and work experience for young people which are run by local training providers. These are aimed at all 16- and 17-year-olds not in school. Places are guaranteed to those who want them. Some people who are a little older are still entitled to a place if they were unable to have one earlier for reasons such as disability or pregnancy. Training is available for those in work as well as those without jobs. Young people who are not working receive a training allowance. Some people also qualify for help with travel, lodgings and other costs. Youth Training (YT) aims to provide vocational education, leading to National Vocational Qualifications (NVQs) at level 2 standard or above.

TECs also offer training for adults. In most cases this is for people who have been unemployed for at least six months. There are exceptions to this: people with a disability; those whose first language is not English and who need language training; people who need training in literacy or numeracy; lone parents who have been on means-tested benefits for more than six months and victims of large-scale redundancies. The scheme is called **Training for Work (TFW)**. Training for Work programmes are intended to meet the needs of the individual and a training adviser works with the person to design a suitable programme. This could include work experience, training and education. People on Training for Work programmes receive a weekly allowance which consists of their normal benefit entitlement plus £10. They may also receive help with the costs of travel and childcare.

Loans to finance courses

Career-development loans (CDLs) are available to help people pay for a course they wish to attend. The loan can be from £200 to £8000. It covers 80 per cent of the fees, and all the expenses of books and other materials and childcare. People who have been out of work for more than three months can apply for a loan to cover 100 per cent of the fees, with the agreement of their local TEC or LEC. The course must be work-related and the loan can cover up to two years' training fees. Courses can be full-time or part-time and living expenses may also be covered for full-time courses.

Repayments on the loan begin one month after the end of the course. If the person is unemployed, payments can be delayed for another five months.

If the course is full-time, it is likely to affect the person's availability for work and therefore make him or her ineligible for benefit. See below for more detail on college courses and benefits entitlement.

Open learning

A relatively recent innovation is **open learning**. This means that students can learn at their own pace, in their own time and without having to attend a college. A package of learning materials is provided, perhaps including books, videos and computer programmes. Sometimes there are support groups. There is a *Directory of Open Learning* which lists the courses that are available. This can be found in libraries. The Open College and the Open University provide college and university courses through **distance learning**.

Colleges

Unemployed people can also enrol on courses at local colleges of further and adult education. Further education colleges are more likely to offer work-related or academic courses leading to qualifications. Adult education colleges are more likely to offer recreational study. This distinction does not always hold true, however; in practice there is a lot of overlap between the two types of colleges.

The Open University allows people to study at home

Some colleges may offer courses specifically for unemployed people, but unemployed people can also join more general courses. Most colleges will offer some kind of reduction in price for people on benefit. Some courses may be free. Grants are also available from the county council. These may cover fees and in some cases other costs as well. Colleges may have a special fund to help people in financial difficulty – perhaps with the cost of books or travel. All these things are worth asking about. Most colleges have student welfare offices which can advise on these and other issues. (See also Chapter 4.)

The effect on benefits

People receiving the Jobseeker's Allowance can study part-time and still receive benefit. People must be available for work and continue to actively look for work. Anyone who is offered a job must not allow their course to prevent them from accepting the job. Courses in further education are counted as part-time if they involve 16 hours or less of 'guided learning'. Colleges can explain what this means in terms of a particular course and indicate whether a course counts as full-time or part-time. For courses in higher education, each course is looked at individually.

WORDCHECK

Training and Education Councils (TECs) Councils in each area, led by local business people, which aim to meet local training needs.

Youth Training (YT) Training for young people; those without jobs receive an allowance.

Training for Work Training for adults; it pays benefits plus £10.

career development loans Loans for training related to work.

open learning Self-study packages which enable people to study without attending a centre.

Finding out more: training and education opportunities

★ Contact the local Training and Enterprise Council (TEC) to discover the local opportunities for training. If the address and phone number are not in *The Phone Book*, ask at the local JobCentre.

★ There may be a computerised database with information on training and educational opportunities. It is called **Training Access Points** (**TAP**) and may be available in the JobCentre or library.

★ See *Just the Job*, a booklet published by the employment service.

★ A leaflet available from social security offices explains the rules about claiming the Jobseeker's Allowance and studying part-time.

★ An excellent and very detailed book called *Unemployment and Training Rights Handbook* by Dan Finn, Iain Murray and Clara Donnelly, is published by the Unemployment Unit.

★ Youthaid publish a *Guide to Training and Benefits for Young People*. It is written by Ianthe Maclagan.

TO FIND OUT

1 Check whether the local library has open-learning materials which can be borrowed.

2 Write to the Open College to find out what is on offer.

TO FIND OUT

Contact local colleges of adult and further education. Find out what is available.

● Are there reductions in fees for people who are unemployed?

● Are there any courses specifically for unemployed people?

● Which courses could people on the Jobseeker's Allowance join without losing their entitlement to benefits?

6.4 Starting a new business

Training and Enterprise Councils (TECs) can provide advice and assistance for people wishing to start a new business. Exactly what is on offer will vary locally to meet local needs.

Business Start Awareness Sessions are run by TECs or agencies contracted to provide the service. They are usually for one day and encourage people who are interested in setting up a business to think about what is involved.

TECs can refer people to enterprise agencies which offer business advice and counselling to provide support in getting going with a new business. There is a free **planning kit** which helps people to design a plan to put to a bank manager or other lender and to avoid unnecessary risks. Short, part-time courses are available to train people in the various skills needed to set up and run a business.

In a few areas of the country, people can apply for an **Enterprise Allowance**. This gives an income until the business gets going. Local TECs decide how long the grant should be for and the amount to be paid. People have to have been unemployed for a while to qualify. A wide variety of schemes have been funded in this way in the past, including counselling services and alternative health care.

Details of all these schemes can be obtained from JobCentres or through the local TEC. (If you cannot find the phone number in *The Phone Book*, ask at the JobCentre.)

6.5 Help with interview expenses

People who have been out of work for more than four weeks can claim financial help from the Travel to Interview Scheme if the job they are applying for is out of their area. Applications must be made before travelling to the interview, and the JobCentre can give full details.

It may be possible for someone on means-tested benefits to obtain a loan from the Social Fund to pay for clothes for an interview, if they do not have suitable clothing.

6.6 People with disabilities – extra help

People with disabilities can make use of any of the programmes and services already described in the chapter. In some cases accelerated entry is possible, but you should check with the JobCentre for up-to-date information on eligibility.

The Disability Discrimination Act

The Disability Discrimination Act 1995, implemented in 1996, makes it illegal for employers with 20 or more staff to discriminate against people with disabilities. The law also means that employers must take reasonable steps to remove physical barriers to employment and to adjust working practices to accommodate people with disabilities. Government funds are available to support some adjustments. Employers should contact the local Placement, Assessment and Counselling Team (PACT) through the Employment Service.

Finding out more: The Disability Discrimination Act

★   RADAR publishes factsheets describing the Disability Discrimination Act.

★   Phone 0345 622633 or write to Disability on the Agenda, FREEPOST, Bristol, BS38 7DE for a copy of the leaflet *A Brief Guide to the Disability Discrimination Act*. Copies are available in large print, braille, audio tape and in a version for people with learning disabilities.

Help with Finding work

The Disability Employment Adviser (DEA) at the JobCentre will offer additional help and support to people who have a health problem that affects their chances of finding or keeping work. This help is available to people looking for work, people who have become disabled while at work and to employers.

The services for people with disabilities include:

- **The Job Introduction Scheme** – this enables people to try a job on a trial basis;
- **The Disability Symbol** – when this is shown on a job advertisement, it indicates that applications from people with disabilities are welcomed by employers who recruit and employ people on the strength of their abilities;
- **Supported employment** – helps people with severe disabilities find and keep a job. This could include supported placements, work in Remploy factories or workshops run by local authorities and voluntary bodies.

Finding out more

★   The Disability Employment Adviser (DEA) at the JobCentre can provide up-to-date information and advice on all aspects of finding and keeping work, and on employing people with disabilities. Look in *The Phone Book* under 'Employment Service' or 'JobCentre'.

6.7 Voluntary work

The emphasis in this chapter is on *paid* employment, but **voluntary work** is an important alternative to paid employment. A voluntary job can provide the same meaning in a person's life as a paid job. Voluntary work gives a sense of purpose and worth, a structure to the day, and social contact with others. Voluntary work is also a way of developing skills and confidence.

Many organisations are desperate for volunteers and it is much easier to find voluntary work than to find a paid job. Many different types of activities are available in many different kinds of settings. There is a much greater likelihood therefore of finding something which fits an individual's particular needs, talents and interests. Hours and times are usually flexible. Many organisations are able to pay expenses and a few pay a little more than this.

Many people who do voluntary work are past retirement age and there is no prejudice about age in the voluntary sector. Similarly, less weight is attached to qualifications and experience than in the competition for paid employment. Voluntary organisations are less likely than many employers to discriminate against someone with a history of mental illness. Although many organisations – especially those involving children – carry out a police check on applicants, this does not mean they will not accept someone with a criminal record. Some people use voluntary work as a way of returning to paid employment, perhaps as a means of gradual return after an illness, or a method of gaining experience. Using voluntary work to gain experience for work or training is especially common in the field of social work. Some

Voluntary work gives a sense of purpose and worth

voluntary organisations provide training courses for their volunteers, and these may lead on to NVQ and other qualifications.

People claiming the Jobseeker's Allowance are allowed to do voluntary work but must still be available for full-time work and take active steps each week to look for work. Claimants are in danger of losing their entitlement to benefit if the voluntary work means they cannot be contacted about a job or cannot start a job within 48 hours. Similarly claimants should not expect to be able to complete a period of voluntary work, even if this seems important to improving their employment prospects. This also could make them ineligible for Jobseeker's Allowance.

TO DO

Think of any clients you have who might be interested in voluntary work.

- What would they gain from voluntary work?
- What skills and experience do they have already?
- Where would you advise them to look for voluntary work?
- Can you anticipate any problems – concerning transport, for instance – and think of solutions?

CASE STUDIES

Imagine you have clients in the following situations. What advice, help and support could you offer?

(a) Mary has not worked since her children were born. Now the youngest has left home, she feels her life is very empty. She is getting depressed. The doctor is reluctant to prescribe drugs and suggests she gets a job.

(b) Tony is 20. He has not worked since he left school, and has been cautioned by police when involved with a group of young men caught trying to break into a shop.

(c) As a result of an accident at work, Harvinder cannot walk. He cannot return to his previous employment, and he cannot stand the idea of doing nothing for the rest of his life. He is 40 years old.

(d) Sheila is a widow who has just retired from a lifetime working, as a schoolteacher and later as a headteacher. Having looked forward to retirement, she now feels lonely and worthless.

7 Children

This chapter looks at the welfare provision which exists to help and protect children. It involves looking at some rather diverse aspects of welfare provision.

The 1989 Children Act

The 1989 Children Act was implemented in 1991. This is an important piece of legislation which covers many aspects of children's welfare. It includes rules on day-care provision, adoption, the care of children after divorce and procedures concerning the protection of children in danger and the care of children being looked after by the local authority. In addition to the Act itself the Department of Health has published a number of volumes of guidance and regulations.

The main principles of the Children Act are:

- the welfare of the child must come first;
- children are best looked after by their families and should only be removed from them when absolutely necessary;
- there should be as little delay as possible in making decisions about children and, where possible, decisions should be made without involving the court;
- local authorities must work in partnership with children and their families;
- parents have a right to a say in what happens to their children;
- parents retain responsibility for their children, even when the children are being looked after by someone else;
- local authorities must help families keep in touch with their children when they are looked after by someone else;
- services must take account of the child's race, religion, culture, language and any disability.

Day care

The first section of this chapter looks at day care for children. Day care can be an important part of a package to help a family. You may see day care as a means of preventing family problems and ultimately of keeping a child out of care. For a mother trying to keep her head above water in difficult circumstances, day care may be an essential lifeline. It gives her vital space for herself or for the other children in the family. Some forms of social services provision take a different approach, aiming to work with the child and parents together. **Family centres** expect parents to attend and work on such areas as parenting skills. You may seek day care for a client where a child has special needs. Specially trained staff can help a child develop his or her full potential. Day care also plays an important part in working with families where there is a risk of **child abuse**. Workers are trained to spot signs of abuse and can also give early warnings of other problems relating to a child's emotional, intellectual or physical development, thereby helping to keep a family together.

Children in danger

The second section of this chapter looks at the protection of children in danger. This is an area which has received a lot of media attention in recent years. There have been a number of very controversial cases and consequent pressure on the government to change the law.

Child abuse is something of a no-win area for social workers. There is still a strong feeling that the family is a private area and that social workers should not interfere. In some of the controversial cases, social workers have been blamed for being too quick to suspect abuse and to remove children from their homes. On the other hand, social workers are also blamed when a child dies from abuse. When they don't react quickly and decisively, they are seen as gullible and too soft on the parents.

Section 7.3 looks at provision available for children in need. This includes care in foster-homes and in residential accommodation, together with services offering support and counselling for children and their families experiencing emotional problems.

The final two sections of the chapter look at the law relating to young offenders and provide an overview of educational provision and rights.

7.1 Day care for children

There is a growing need for day care for children. Clients may want day care for a variety of reasons. More women are wanting paid employment, even when their children are small. Women who do not have paid jobs still feel that their children benefit from the different experiences they have in nurseries and playgroups. Families are smaller these days, and many children do not have sisters or brothers to play with at home. Nurseries and playgroups have bigger and more varied toys than many parents could afford. They can allow messy and wet play without worrying about the housework involved. Many of the staff are trained in play methods and in child development. They may have more imaginative ideas for play. Nurseries and playgroups also play an important role in preparing children for school. Children will have experienced leaving their parents for short periods and be used to a different environment and to a day which is more structured than at home.

This country provides less in the way of day care than do many other European countries. As a result much of the provision is privately offered – mostly by childminders, working in their own homes. Although many parents use childminders, this is not their preferred option. Workplace or other nurseries are more popular, but these are few and far between. Where they do exist, they are often too expensive for parents to afford. This section examines the various types of child care available.

The duties of local authorities

Provision of child care

Although local authorities do not have to meet all parents' needs for child care, they do have certain duties in this area. The 1989 Children Act states that local authority social services departments, in association with local education authorities, must review day-care services for children under the age of eight. This includes services provided by the local authority as well as those provided by childminders and other private and voluntary organisations. The review must be carried out at least every three years and the results published.

The Act also gives local authorities the duty to provide day-care services for children in need. This includes children up to five, and those up to 16 after school hours and in the school holidays. Need is defined in two ways. It includes children with disabilities; and children who are unlikely to achieve or maintain a reasonable standard of health and development, or who would not do so without special provision. Examples of services could be day nurseries, places in playgroups, a place with a childminder or an out-of-school club. Local authorities may provide services for other children as well, but the government does not require them to do so.

Registration of child-care services

The other major responsibility of the local authority social services department in this area is the **registration** of private and voluntary child-care services. Anyone who provides day care for children up to the age of eight for more than two hours a day must be registered. This includes shared nannies, employed by more than two families.

Before the childminder, nursery or playgroup can be registered, the social services department must decide on their 'fitness'. This has two aspects. First, the minder must be a 'fit' person to care for children, as must any other person living or working on the premises. Secondly, the premises themselves must also be fit.

The Department of Health has issued guidance on standards for local authorities to look for in terms of 'fitness'. These cover the facilities and equipment available and child-care practice. Most local authorities have policies on smacking and other forms of physical punishment of children but these have proved difficult to enforce in practice. The local authority will also consider the experience, qualifications and multi-cultural awareness of the minder. The local authority will set conditions such as the number of children allowed in the group or to be minded, safety measures which must be taken and details of required record-keeping. Other conditions can be added. The authority must inspect at least once a year. Fees are charged for this at a rate set by the government.

The 1989 Children Act emphasised the need for an anti-racist and multi-cultural approach to child care. Registration can be cancelled if the care given to an individual child is thought to be seriously inadequate in terms of the child's religion, racial origin, or cultural and linguistic background.

Day nurseries

There are places in **day nurseries** for about two per cent of all children under the age of five. Many local authorities provide day nurseries, but the type of provision varies a great deal from area to area.

In some large towns day care is provided for working parents. In other places the service is in the form of **family centres**. Family centres do not usually take children if the parents are working and places are allocated on the basis of need. The children who are accepted will have special needs or be thought to be at risk or deprived in some way.

There are also nurseries that are run privately. These tend to be expensive. Some employers provide **workplace nurseries** for their staff. It is predicted that this form of provision might increase in the future as employers try to attract women workers. Universities and colleges sometimes provide nursery facilities also, for both staff and students. These college and workplace nurseries are popular since only one journey is involved each day for the parent and the child, and the child is close by and can be visited at lunchtimes.

Nurseries are usually open long hours, to accommodate working parents.

Childminders

Childminders are legally required to register with the local authority. Although it is hard to estimate figures, it is likely, however, that there are people minding who are *not* registered. The delays sometimes put people off; so does the fear that they might be refused registration, or limited in the number of children they can take.

There has been a recent increase in the numbers of childminders. This has put a considerable strain on social services resources. Long waiting lists for registration are common. More pressure has resulted from the 1989 Children Act, which brought in the need for childminders with children under the age of eight to register. (Previously the age was five.)

Most childminders work privately, although a few local authorities have salaried childminders working for them. More commonly, some children will be subsidised by the local authority. Childminders are usually women with young children of their own who want a way of earning extra money without going out to work. Social services hold lists of registered childminders which can be used by someone looking for a childminder.

Standards of childminding vary tremendously, from women who provide excellent care to those with poor facilities and little understanding of children's needs. Some local authorities provide training and support groups for childminders, but this is fairly minimal. There is a national organisation for childminders which provides information and support.

One of the few things available to all childminders is free milk: registered childminders are entitled to receive one-third of a pint of milk per day for each child minded.

Finding out more: *childminding*

★ For information on childminding, contact the *National Childminding Association*. The Association has local groups which share ideas and provide support. Membership entitles childminders to an insurance policy and a newsletter. NCMA also provides advice, information and leaflets.

The National Childminding Association can provide information for parents and childminders

Playgroups

About half of all children aged three or four attend **playgroups**. They usually attend two or three sessions a week for a couple of hours only. Since the hours are so short, parents cannot use playgroups as a means of child care to allow them to work. Some children are, however, taken to playgroups by their childminders.

Playgroups have to register with social services, who expect playgroup supervisors to have had some training. Training is on a part-time basis: it is provided by the *Pre-School Learning Alliance*, but financed by the county council. The majority of playgroups are affiliated to the Pre-School Learning Alliance. Playgroups encourage parents to be involved, and many of the helpers are parents of playgroup children. Many playgroups will take children with special needs and sometimes social services provide extra support in these cases.

Finding out more: playgroups

★ For information on playgroups, contact the Pre-School Learning Alliance. It provides information on playgroups and on starting a playgroup. Through a system of regional and area fieldworkers, the Pre-School Learning Alliance supports local playgroups.

Nursery schools and classes

About a quarter of three- and four-year-olds attend a **nursery school** or **nursery class**. Most of the children are in their pre-school year and most attend part-time – either mornings or afternoons. Although the emphasis in nursery schools is still on play, the time is likely to be more structured than in a playgroup, to prepare the children for school.

Vouchers

From April 1997 all parents of four-year-old children will receive a voucher which can be used to pay part or all of the cost of three terms of pre-school education at a **validated institution**. Validated institutions include playgroups run by voluntary organisations, nursery classes and schools provided by the local authority and private facilities. Validation requires that providers are registered under the Children Act, are inspected regularly and work towards educational objectives set by the Schools Curriculum and Assessment Authority (SCAA). For local authority places, the voucher will cover the full cost, but parents can top up the amount in more expensive nurseries.

Care for school-age children

For working parents, the problem of child care does not end when the child starts school at five. Very few jobs fit in exactly with school hours and holidays. Most children of working parents are cared for by relatives or childminders. There are, however, a few out-of-school schemes for children after school hours and in the holidays. These usually use the school premises, and tend to be found in large cities.

Most playgroups are affiliated to the Pre-School Learning Alliance

---

TO DO

Survey clients on their preferences for child care. Compare working and non-working parents.

Ask about the child care used currently and in the past, and ask people what they would actually *like* to be available.

Many children attend playgroups

TO FIND OUT

What facilities are there for child care in your local area?

- Does the local authority provide any day nurseries? If so, on what basis are children accepted?
- Are there any private nurseries?
- Do any local employers provide child care?
- Does the local college have a crèche?
- Find out from social services how many childminders there are in the area. Contact one or two, to compare the costs.

- What playgroups are there? What ages of children do they take? Would they take children with physical or learning disabilities?
- Are there any nursery schools? Which primary schools have nursery classes?
- Are there any facilities for school-age children after school and in the holidays?

CASE STUDIES

Imagine you have clients in the following situations. What help, advice and support would you offer?

(a) Shelley is 17 and unmarried. She lives alone in a flat with her one-year-old baby. She loves the baby and has coped so far, but now the child is becoming more active she is finding things more difficult. She is lonely in her flat and showing signs of depression.

(b) Clare and Stephen's third child, Peter, has Down's syndrome. Sally is very protective of Peter and does

not allow any rough-and-tumble play. The others in the family, including Tom, seem jealous of the amount of attention Sally gives to Peter.

(c) Wendy abused her first child, who is now with foster parents. She is about to give birth to her second child. Her circumstances are now different, in that the father of the second child is supportive. Wendy is frightened that she will lose this child and wants help.

7.2 The law protecting children

The 1989 Children Act aimed to pull together several older Acts and to simplify the law. Under the Act, local authorities have a duty to protect children in their area. This duty is carried out by the social workers in the social services departments. Although the law does not say how local authorities must organise their service, they are bound to provide services which prevent children from being the victims of ill-treatment or neglect. If it is suspected that a child may be in danger, the local authority is bound, under law, to investigate the situation.

There are also voluntary organisations working in the area of child protection. The *National Society for the Prevention of Cruelty to Children* (NSPCC) plays an important role in this area. Its inspectors work in a similar way to social services social workers, often in close liaison. They can be involved in all the court proceedings described below. *Childline* is a telephone helpline for children themselves if they are in trouble. Calls are free and are answered by trained counsellors.

Childline is a telephone helpline for children in trouble

The law

The law provides for a number of different **court orders** which give social workers powers to intervene in families. An aim of the law is to balance the interests of parents, children and the authorities – whilst always having the welfare of the child as the *first* consideration.

In a situation where social workers are concerned for the welfare of a child, they do not *have* to take the child into care. The social worker may feel that it would be damaging for a child to be taken from his or her home. If the child is not felt to be in danger, he or she may be left at home. Social services can provide support in the home – perhaps the services of a family home help, or the support of a social worker. They can also provide money if this will help the situation. The law also provides that help – in the form of different housing, for instance – could be given to someone else in the household, for example someone who is suspected of abusing the child. However, these decisions must always be made with the *child's* interests and safety as the main consideration.

Child assessment order

If the social workers feel that a child is at risk at home they must investigate the situation. They must then apply for one of the court orders available or decide to review the situation at a later date.

There have been situations in the past where social workers have not been able to get access to examine a child they were worried about. To stop this happening again, there is now a **child assessment order**. The court will give this order if it feels that there is a suspicion of significant harm to the child, but no immediate emergency. A child assessment order lasts for seven days. It can include the child being taken from the home for examination if this is thought to be necessary. A child who is the subject of a child assessment order has the right to refuse to be examined.

Emergency protection order

An **emergency protection order** can be granted if the court feels that the child is likely to suffer significant harm if he or she is left at home or allowed to go home. It lasts for seven days and can be extended for a further seven days. The police have the power to remove a child straightaway, but they must then inform the local authority. This is for a period of 72 hours, and the parents must be allowed to see the child.

Care order

A **care order** brings the child into the care of the local authority. It gives parental responsibility for the child to the local authority. With a care order the child would normally be removed from home: the child may live with foster parents or in a community home run by the local authority or a voluntary organisation. (A *supervision order* – see below – is similar but allows the child to remain at home.)

The fact that the local authority has parental responsibility does not remove responsibility from the parents (or the people looking after the child). It is the *prime* responsibility only that goes to the local authority. The law encourages parents to continue to be involved with the child, and local authorities are expected to look for ways to share responsibility. The grounds for a care order or a supervision order are:

The 1989 Children Act provides the framework for child protection

- that the child is suffering or is likely to suffer significant harm; *and*
- that the harm is because *either* (a) the care given by the parents is not what it is reasonable to expect, *or* (b) the child is beyond the control of the parents.

A care order will not be made unless the court considers that making an order is a better option than not doing so. This requirement is known as the 'presumption of no order'.

Supervision order

With a **supervision order**, the child remains at home and has a social worker whose role is to advise, help and befriend. The child and the parent must make sure the social worker is aware of any moves of house and can meet the child. It may be that the child is required to live at a particular place or has to join in some organised activities.

Interim care order

It is also possible for an **interim care order** to be made, if the full hearing cannot take place for some reason. This lasts for up to eight weeks, and a second one can only last for four weeks.

Guardian ad litem

There is a system whereby an adult is appointed to represent the interests of the child in court. This person is called a **guardian *ad litem*.** It is the duty of the court to appoint such a person unless the court is satisfied that it is not necessary to do so. The guardian *ad litem* carries out an investigation, interviewing various people such as the child himself or herself, social workers, parents and relatives. A report is then presented to the court which tries to state what actions are in the best interests of the child.

Case conferences

As was mentioned earlier, the law does not state how the social services departments must act to prevent child abuse. The usual system is through multi-disciplinary committees and **case conferences**. These bring together all the different people who might be involved with a particular child. Knowledge is shared and a decision made as to the best course of action. The people involved are likely to include social workers, police officers, a member of staff from the school, GPs, and other health-care workers such as health visitors. There may also be workers from the National Society for Prevention of Cruelty to Children if they also are involved with the case.

Working Together

In 1991 the government published *Working Together Under the Children Act 1989*. For some years government policy has stressed the need for agencies concerned with children to co-operate in helping children at risk of harm. These agencies include social service departments, doctors, the police, health visitors, schools and local voluntary organisations. *Working Together Under the Children Act 1989* gives guidance on how agencies should work together, keeping parents informed and involved. The child-care agencies must form a Child Protection Committee. The Committee will decide guidelines on procedures to be followed in individual child protection cases. The procedures will be monitored and reviewed and recommendations made in response to new cases, reports or enquiries about child protection.

Case conferences bring together all the people involved with a particular child

'At risk' registers

Each area keeps a register of children who have been abused or who are suspected of having been abused. This is looked after either by the local authority or by the NSPCC.

Other local authority involvement

It is possible for a child to be **looked after** by the local authority without being in care. This happens in situations where the local authority is providing a home for a child without there being a court order. Social services must provide for children who have no one to look after them, who are lost or abandoned, or whose carer is unable – temporarily or permanently – to provide care. The child's wishes in such a situation should be considered and the parents are allowed to take the child back without any notice.

The local authority has a duty to help contact between the parents and the child. This can include paying the costs of visits to the child. There must also be regular reviews of the situations of all children being looked after by the local authority.

WORDCHECK

voluntary organisation An organisation which has not been set up by a government body and which does not aim to make a profit.

helpline A telephone counselling or information service.

child assessment order A court order which allows social workers access to a child whom they suspect might be being abused.

emergency protection order A court order which gives social workers the right to remove a child who is felt to be in danger.

care order A court order which brings a child into the care of the local authority.

supervision order A court order whereby a child lives at home but has a social worker as adviser and counsellor.

interim care order A temporary care order when a full court hearing is not possible.

guardian *ad litem* An adult who represents a vulnerable person's interests in the court.

case conference A multi-disciplinary meeting to share ideas about a social work case.

'at risk' register A list of children who are thought to be at risk of child abuse.

Finding out more: the 1989 Children Act

★   The Children Act 1989 is a very complex piece of legislation. A useful and jargon-free guide is *Making Sense of the Children Act* (second edition) by Nick Allen, published by Longman (Harlow, 1992).

★   The National Children's Bureau provides a catalogue of books on various issues affecting children.

★   The Department of Health produces a set of leaflets on the Children Act.

★   A useful book on all aspects of law relating to care work is *Law for Social Workers* (fourth edition) by Hugh Brayne and Gerry Martin, published by Blackstone Press.

7.3 Provision for children in need

Services for children in need are provided by social services departments and by voluntary and private organisations. Social services are responsible for inspection and registration of facilities provided by the independent sector. Where necessary, social services will pay for a child to be cared for in a home run by a private or voluntary organisation.

Social services vary from area to area in the provision they make for children in need of support or care. It is, however, a general policy that where possible children should be cared for in a family environment. Gone are the days of large institutional orphanages, so the first aim would be for a child to be cared for in his or her own home, perhaps with the support of family home helps and social workers. There are also various day centres which provide counselling, therapy and support.

The 1989 Children Act allows local authorities to provide accommodation for children on a voluntary basis to help families in difficulties. The intention of the Act is that this should be seen positively, as a means of helping the child, not as a sign of parental failure or family breakdown. Such voluntary use of local authority services is described as being 'accommodated'.

Where children are compulsorily placed with foster parents or in residential accommodation, this must be done under a care order from the court, as described in the previous section of this chapter.

Foster parents

If the child could not remain with his or her immediate family or with relatives, **foster parents** would be looked for. These are people, not necessarily trained, who care for children in their own home. This may be a short-term or a long-term arrangement. Foster parents who apply are carefully vetted. If accepted, they are paid an allowance for each child in their care. Fostering does not always work out; it is quite common for fostering arrangements to break down, especially with older or very disturbed children. Entering a new family can be a very emotionally demanding and stressful situation for a child. Voluntary organisations such as *Barnardo's* also run fostering schemes, sometimes specialising in working with children with special needs.

Residential accommodation

Sometimes a family situation is not possible or suitable for a child. In such a case the child can be placed in **residential accommodation**. Social services homes for children are usually small, and appear very much like ordinary houses. They are run by **house parents** and a team of other staff. The staff will probably not live on the premises but there will be facilities for staff to sleep over at nights. There are children's homes run by voluntary organisations, too, such as the *National Children's Homes* (NCH). Private organisations also run children's homes, and these are used by social services departments when necessary.

Other services

Social services and voluntary organisations may provide various other services such as day centres and support services. **Child-guidance clinics** are usually administered by the local education authority. The staff working in the clinics are employed by various different authorities, however: there will be **social workers** from the social services department, and **psychotherapists** and **psychiatrists** from the health authority. **Educational psychologists** may also work in the clinic. Child-guidance clinics work with children and families where there are emotional problems. The work is usually long-term, with weekly meetings.

WORDCHECK

voluntary organisation An organisation which has not been set up by a government body and which does not aim to make a profit.

child-guidance clinic A service which provides therapy and counselling for families and children with emotional and psychological problems.

care order A court order which brings a child into the care of the local authority.

looked after Children are described as being looked after by the local authority when they are in care, or when they have been provided with accommodation for more than 24 hours.

accommodated Children who are accommodated by the local authority are not in care, but are receiving help on a voluntary basis.

Finding out more: voluntary organisations

★ *Barnardo's* provides a number of services for children in need. It runs a fostering service and specialises in working with children with learning disabilities. It has residential centres and hostels. It supports young people and families in the community, and has day-care centres for under-fives.

★ *The Children's Legal Centre* provides a free advice and information service by letter or telephone. The centre also publishes leaflets.

★ The *Family Rights Group* advises families on child protection issues or with children being accommodated or supported by the local authority. The Group has lists of solicitors able to act in care proceedings and can prepare reports for use in court.

★ *The National Society for the Prevention of Cruelty to Children* (*NSPCC*) works to prevent harm to children and publishes information on its work.

★ *NCH Action for Children* provides a range of innovative services for children including various projects in the community and residential accommodation.

TO FIND OUT

1 Contact the county council or the local social services department to find out what the local policy is on caring for children in need.

2 What services are offered locally for children and young people? Start with social services, but consider also any privately-run facilities or those offered by voluntary organisations.

7.4 Young offenders

In law a child has to be 10 before he or she can commit a crime. If a child aged between 10 and 14 commits a crime, it must be shown to the court that the child knew that what he or she was doing was wrong. Between the ages of 14 and 17 a child is capable of committing a crime, but will be classed as a youth and dealt with under the youth justice system.

Young offenders appear before the **youth court**. This may be in the same building as the magistrate's court, but it is otherwise quite separate and there are different principles and rules. The main principle is that the welfare of the child must be considered as well as the offence. Children are seen as products of their home and social environment, and as in need of help rather than punishment. The court will receive reports from social workers and probation officers. These people look at the home and family, report on schooling, and examine many other aspects of the child's personality and life. Social workers play an important role in working with young offenders. As well as producing reports for the court, they are responsible for supervision orders (see below). They work with young offenders to try to prevent re-offending. In some areas this work is done through **youth justice centres**. These provide a range of activities to help young people in trouble.

The police usually deal with young people through their **Community Services Branch (CSB)**. They follow the **Police and Criminal Evidence Act 1984 Codes of Practice** when dealing with young offenders. This requires that 'the appropriate adult' be contacted and be present when a young offender is being interviewed. The appropriate adult would normally be a parent, but could be a social worker or some other person. He or she should not be a police officer.

The police deal with young people through their Community Services Branch

In some cases, the police will **caution** a young person whom they have caught committing a crime. This is a serious and formal warning which prevents the young person from getting into the justice system. A previous caution can be mentioned if a young person is later sentenced for a subsequent offence. A caution can only be given if the young person admits to the crime and if the parents agree to this procedure.

Community service can be used as an alternative to custody

Finding out more: rights at police stations

★   For more detailed information on rights at police stations and other aspects of the law, see *Law for Social Workers* by Hugh Brayne and Gerry Martin (Blackstone Press: fourth edition, 1995).

The youth court

The courts have a number of options when considering the case of a young offender. As mentioned earlier, the court will look at the whole situation – not just the offence – in deciding the best course of action. For example, it would be possible for several youngsters involved in the same offence each to receive different treatment. The rest of this section lists the various options open to the youth court.

Custody

A custodial sentence is one in which a young offender is sent either to a **Young Offender Institution** or a **Secure Training Centre**. This is the most serious sentence a court can give. Secure Training Orders were introduced under the Criminal Justice and Public Order Act 1994. They allow for persistent offenders aged 12–14 years to be placed in privately run Secure Training Centres. Offenders aged 15–17 years are sent to Young Offender Institutions. People can only be sent to institutions in situations where either the offence is so serious that this is the only sentence which can be justified or where it is a violent or sexual offence for which the sentence is necessary to protect the public. Giving a young offender a custodial sentence is a last resort for the court. It would be unlikely to happen in the case of a first offence.

Community service order

Under a **community service order** the offender must spend some time working in the community. The young person must be 16 and must agree to the order. As with custody, the crime must be one for which an adult would be imprisoned. The minimum amount of time which can be given is 40 hours and the maximum is 240 hours.

Fine

A young offender can be fined. The maximum **fine** for a 10–13-year-old is £250 and the maximum for a 14–17-year-old is £1000. The court will look at the young person's ability to pay – the child's, rather than the parents – and the fine can be paid in instalments.

Supervision order

This means the offender must work with a supervisor from social services or the probation service. The role of the supervisor is to befriend and advise.

The supervision order can last up to three years. Restrictions can be attached. These include having to live in local authority accommodation, having to live with a particular person (usually a relative), having to join in supervised activities, and being prevented from going out at certain times. This last – a **curfew** – may, for example, prevent someone who has caused trouble at football matches from attending any such matches. This type of restriction can apply only for the first 90 days.

Binding parents over

This means the parent or guardian promises to take care of the child and to exercise proper control to try to stop the young person re-offending. A sum of money is agreed – to a maximum £1000 – which will be forfeited if the young person commits a further crime. There is a maximum period of three years, and the order cannot go past the young person's 18th birthday.

Attendance centre

This is another decision which can be made only if the crime is one for which an adult could be imprisoned. The young offender must turn up at the attendance centre for a period of between 12 and 24 hours. Attendance centres are usually run by the police and held in schools or youth clubs. Commonly, they are held for two hours each Saturday.

Compensation order

The offender can be told to **compensate** the victim of the crime. This can be the only punishment, or it can be given with other sentences. Account must be taken of the young person's ability to pay.

Probation

Offenders can be given a probation order if they are 16 or older and have committed a crime serious enough to warrant such an order. The probation order involves supervision by a probation officer for a period of between six months and three years. The offender must keep in touch with the probation officer and extra requirements can also be attached to the order. Examples of requirements are having to live at a particular address or having to undergo treatment for drug or alcohol addiction.

Combination orders

For offenders aged 16 and over these allow a combination of probation and a community service order. The number of hours of the community service is between 40 and 100.

Deferred sentence

If something is about to change in the offender's life – perhaps a new job or a change of school – the court may decide to delay making a decision until afterwards. The delay can only be for six months and the young person must agree with the plan.

Discharge

It is possible for the court to decide that no punishment is appropriate. An **absolute discharge** means that the offence is ignored for all purposes except sentencing for any *future* offence. A **conditional discharge** can be given for up to three years. If the person commits a further offence, he or she will be sentenced for the original offence *as well as* the later one which the court is then considering.

WORDCHECK

youth court The court which deals with young offenders.

supervision order A court order whereby a child lives at home but has a social worker as adviser and counsellor.

Community Services Branch (CSB) A branch of the police which deals with young people and others thought to be vulnerable.

caution A formal warning given by the police, without a case going to court.

community service order A sentence which means that the offender has to work in the community for a set number of hours.

binding parents over A court order which requires parents or guardians to control a young offender.

attendance centre Provision for young offenders, usually run by the police on Saturdays.

deferred sentence Sentencing is delayed until a specified date.

absolute discharge No sentence is given.

conditional discharge An offender will be sentenced for the given offence only if he or she commits another offence.

compensation order A court order which requires an offender to compensate the victim of the crime.

Young Offender Institution Centres for young offenders aged between 15 and 17 years.

Secure Training Centres Institutions for persistent offenders aged 12 to 14 years.

probation order Offenders aged 16 or over are supervised by a probation officer.

combination orders For offenders aged 16 or over, this allows a combination of probation and a community service order.

TO DO

Think about the following situations and decide what you think the police or the court should do. If you think you need more information, what do you want to know?

Make the decision first using the list of possible options open to the court (pages 138–40). Then consider whether there is anything you would rather decide, if you were free to impose *any* punishment or treatment.

(a) A boy of 10 steals a toy from a shop. The home situation is that his mother and father have recently split up. The child does not show any sign of being particularly upset by this, however.

(b) Three boys, aged 10, 12 and 15, burn down a barn. The 15-year-old has already been to court for a similar offence and is currently going to an attendance centre. His parents are divorced and he lives with his father. The father is rarely at home: he works shifts and likes to go to the pub when he is not working nights. The other two are brothers and have no previous history of offending. They have recently moved to the area. Their parents seem to look after them well.

(c) Two boys of 16 attack and injure another boy of the same age. The boy who is attacked is white and has been insulting and bullying younger Asian children in school. The boys who injure him are Asian. None of the boys has any previous history of offending. The Asians are successful in school and about to start A-levels; the white boy is regarded by the school as a troublemaker.

(d) Four 15-year-old girls have been caught with drugs. The drugs are cannabis and LSD. Three of the girls have only small amounts of the drugs, although one has been cautioned already when cannabis was found previously. The others have no history of offending. One of the girls is found to have a large quantity of drugs in her bedroom. The police suspect she has been dealing, but there is no other evidence for this. All the girls come from well-off families, but they are regarded by their families and schools as 'quite rebellious' and difficult. All are doing well at school, however, and the one with the large quantity of drugs is expected to do very well.

(e) A boy of 16 has a record of 20 other offences. These are for various crimes, including stealing, taking and driving away of cars, and assault. He is unemployed and lives with his mother and step-father. His real father is in prison. The current offence involved breaking into a house and stealing a video.

Finding out more: youth justice

★ A useful book on all aspects of law relating to care work is *Law for Social Workers* (fourth edition) by Hugh Brayne and Gerry Martin, published by Blackstone Press, 1995.

★ Blackstone Press also publish very detailed guides to legislation. There is a *Guide to The Criminal Justice Act 1991* by Martin Wasik and Richard D. Taylor (second edition, 1994).

7.5 Rights to education

All children have a right to education from the age of 5 to the age of 16. Beyond 16 there is further and higher education for those who choose to stay on and who have the qualifications needed for particular courses. Education is free for children aged between 5 and 16 in schools maintained by the local education authority (**county schools**) and in **grant-maintained schools**. Grant-maintained schools are funded directly from central government and run by a governing body. **Independent schools** are outside the state education system and parents pay for their children to attend. Some independent schools have joined the **assisted places scheme** which allows parents on low incomes with children in independent schools to qualify for help with the cost of the fees.

There is a Charter explaining parents' rights in schools

In some cases local education authorities provide grants for help with the costs of school uniforms or other clothing or footwear. Children who go to their nearest school will qualify for free travel if the school is too far away for walking. There may also be help from the local authority with the cost of school trips. See Chapter 4 for information on grants for education beyond the age of 16.

Parents' choice

Parents have the right to choose a school for their children and the school must take the children if there are places. The only exceptions to this are selective schools and Church schools which can select children. Local education authorities and grant-maintained schools must publish information to help parents make a choice – this must include information on disciplinary policies and examination results.

The national curriculum

There is a **national curriculum** for all children aged 5 to 16 in maintained schools. This includes three core subjects: English, mathematics and science. Welsh is a core subject in schools where Welsh is spoken. The compulsory foundation subjects are: technology, history, geography, art, music, physical education. A foreign language is compulsory for pupils aged 11 to 16 and Welsh is a foundation subject in non-Welsh speaking schools in Wales. Schooling is divided into four **key stages** which cover the ages 5–7, 7–11, 11–14, 14–16. **Programmes of study** are set for each key stage and there are **attainment targets** which set standards for pupils' performances. Pupils are assessed at the end of each of the key stages.

Exclusion from school

In some situations, children are **excluded** from school because of their behaviour. The 1993 Education Act allows for two types of exclusion.

- A **fixed term exclusion** – a child is excluded for a set number of school days. A child cannot be excluded for more than a total of 15 days in a term.
- A **permanent exclusion**.

Certain principles and procedures must be followed when a school is deciding to exclude a pupil. Parents must be told about the exclusion as soon as possible and preferably on the same day. Parents are entitled to say what they think about the exclusion to the school governors and to appeal against the decision.

Special needs

The 1981 Education Act was updated by the 1993 Education Act. The 1993 Act requires all maintained schools to do their best to provide for children's special educational needs. Local education authorities have a duty to identify children whose needs cannot be met by mainstream provision and to make an assessment of such children's needs. This assessment will involve a number of professionals and take account of medical, educational, psychological and any other relevant factors. If the assessment indicates that the child's needs are such that the local authority needs to decide what provision should be made, then the authority is required to make a **statement** of special educational needs. Parents can appeal against the statement to an independent tribunal. The government have produced a Code of Practice which sets out guidance for local authorities on assessments and statements.

As far as possible children with special needs must be educated in ordinary schools. The 1993 Education Act gives parents of children with statements the right to say which school they would prefer their child to attend. The authority must go along with the parents' wishes, subject to the suitability of the school and the efficient use of resources.

Local authorities have a duty to provide for children with statements who are over the age of two and statements can continue until the young

---

TO FIND OUT

1 Find out about local policy on children with learning disabilities. First contact the local education authority to discover its policy.

2 Contact a few primary and secondary schools to find out whether they would accept a child with a learning disability. Use specific examples, for instance a child who is blind, a child with cerebral palsy and in a wheelchair, and a child with Down's syndrome. Compare the responses of the primary and secondary schools.

3 Contact the local college of further education to see what facilities are available there.

person is 19. There are increasing numbers of students with special needs in colleges of further and higher education.

TO THINK ABOUT

What is the best way to educate children with learning disabilities?

- What are the advantages and the disadvantages of educating children with learning disabilities within mainstream schools?
- Do you have any personal experience of learning disabilities, such as may result from Down's syndrome, blindness or inability to walk? What recommendations would *you* make?

The local education authority must identify and assess children with special educational needs

CASE STUDIES

Imagine you have clients in the following situations. What advice, help and support would you give?

(a) Pam is worried about her daughter, aged eight. Marie seems slow to learn and is already behind the other children at school in reading and writing.

(b) James is 13 and very disruptive at school. He has been suspended several times and the headteacher is suggesting that he should not remain at the school.

(c) Robert is 11 and has cerebral palsy. So far he has been educated in an ordinary primary school. Now there is a choice between a large comprehensive school, with little in the way of special facilities, and a special school for children with physical disabilities. This has a good reputation but would entail a long journey.

WORDCHECK

county schools Schools which are provided and maintained by the local education authority.

grant-maintained schools Schools which have voted to leave the control of the local education authority and receive funding direct from central government and be self-governing.

independent schools Schools which are run privately and financed through fees paid by parents.

national curriculum Programmes of study set by the government for all children in maintained schools.

key stages Stages of education at the end of which children are assessed against national standards.

assisted places scheme A scheme which pays the fees for children at independent schools whose parents are on a low income.

statement A statement by the local authority of provision to be made for a child with special educational needs.

Finding out more: educational rights

★ For detailed information on exclusion, special needs and all other aspects of educational rights, contact: The Advisory Centre for Education (ACE).

★ A series of charters is available explaining rights to education. These can be obtained from the Department for Education and Employment. Many educational institutions also have their own charters or handbooks.

★ For a list of government publications on education, contact the Department for Education and Employment (address in the appendix).

★ For information on independent schools, write or phone the Independent Schools Information Service (ISIS).

★ Information about courses in further and higher education can be obtained from the Education and Counselling Credit Transfer Information Service (ECCTIS).

Appendix: useful addresses and helplines

Addresses

ADFAM National 5th Floor, Epworth House, 25 City Road, London EC1Y 1AA. *Tel.* 0171 638 3700; *Fax* 0171 256 6320.

Advisory Centre for Education (ACE) 1B Aberdeen Studios, 22 Highbury Grove, London N5 2DQ. *Tel.* 0171 354 8318; *Fax* 0171 354 9069.

Age Concern England Astral House, 1268 London Road, London SW16 4ER. *Tel.* 0181 679 8000; *Fax* 0181 679 6069.

AIDS Education and Research Trust (AVERT) 11–13 Denne Parade, Horsham, West Sussex RH12 1JD. *Tel.* 01403 210202.

Al-Anon Family Groups 61 Great Dover Street, London SE1 4YF. *Tel.* 0171 403 0888; *Fax* 0171 378 9910.

Alcohol Concern Waterbridge House, 32–36 Loman Street, London SE1 0EE. *Tel.* 0171 928 7377; *Wales:* 01222 488000.

Alcoholics Anonymous Head Office, PO Box 1, Stonebow House, Stonebow, York YO1 2NJ. *Tel.* 01904 644026; London: 0171 352 3001; Wales: 01222 373939; Northern Ireland: 01232 681084; Scotland: 0141 221 9027.

Alternative Health Information Bureau 12 Upper Station Road, Radlett, Herts WD7 8BX. *Tel.* 01923 469495; *Fax* 01923 857670.

Association of Community Health Councils Earlsmead House, 30 Drayton Park, London N5 1PB. *Tel.* 0171 609 8405; *Fax* 0171 700 1152.

Association of Therapeutic Communities Pine Street Day Centre, 13–15 Pine Street, London EC1R 01H. *Tel./Fax* 0181 950 9557.

BACUP (British Association of Cancer United Patients) 3 Bath Place, Rivington Street, London EC2A 3JR. *Tel.* Cancer Information Service Freeline 0800 181199 or Cancer Counselling Service 0171 696 9000; *Fax* 0171 696 9002.

Bailey Distribution Ltd (CPA) Learoyd Road, New Romney, Kent TN28 8XU. *Tel.* 01797 369966.

Barnardo's Tanners Lane, Barkingside, Ilford, Essex IG6 1QG. *Tel.* 0181 550 8822; *Fax* 0181 551 6870.

Blackliners Eurolink Business Centre, 49 Effra Road, London SW2 1BZ. Helpline *Tel.* 0171 738 5274.

Bristol Cancer Help Centre Grove House, Cornwallis Grove, Clifton, Bristol B58 4PG. *Tel.* 0117 973 0500; *Fax* 0117 923 9184.

British Acupuncture Council, The Park House, 206–208 Latimer Road, London W10 6RE. *Tel.* 0181 964 0222; *Fax* 0181 964 0333.

British Airports Authority (BAA) Jubilee House, Furlong Way, North Terminal, Gatwick Airport (London), West Sussex RH6 0JN. *Tel.* 01293 517755; *Fax* 01293 595885.

British Association for Counselling (BAC) 1 Regent Place, Rugby, Warwickshire CV21 2PJ. *Tel.* 01788 578328; *Fax* 01788 562189.

British Association of Psychotherapists 37 Mapesbury Road, London NW2 4HJ. *Tel.* 0181 452 9823; *Fax* 0181 452 5182.

British Chiropractic Association 29 Whitley Street, Reading, Berkshire RG2 0EG. *Tel.* 01734 757557; *Fax* 01734 757257.

British Complementary Medicine Association 39 Prestbury Road, Cheltenham, Gloucestershire GL52 2PT. *Tel.* 01242 226770; *Fax* 01242 267708.

British Dental Association 64 Wimpole Street, London W1M 8AL. *Tel.* 0171 935 0875; *Fax* 0171 487 5732.

British Dental Health Foundation Eastlands Court, St Peter's Road, Rugby, Warwickshire CV21 3QP. *Tel.* 01788 546365; *Fax* 01788 546365.

British Medical Acupuncture Association Newton House, Newton Lane, Whitley, Warrington, Cheshire WA4 4JA. *Tel.* 01925 730727; *Fax* 01925 730492.

British Homeopathic Association 27A Devonshire Street, London W1N 1RJ. *Tel.* 0171 935 2163.

British Pregnancy Advisory Service (BPAS) Head Office, Austy Manor, Wootton Waven, Solihull, West Midlands B95 6BX. *Tel.* 01564 793225; *Fax* 01564 794935.

British Sports Association for Disabled People Solecast House, 13–27 Brunswick Place, London N1 6DX. *Tel.* 0171 490 4919.

British Wireless for the Blind Fund Gabriel House, 34 New Road, Chatham, Kent ME4 4QR. *Tel.* 01634 832501.

Brook Advisory Centres 165 Gray's Inn Road, London WC1X 8UD. *Tel.* 0171 713 9000 and 0171 833 8488.

Cancer Care Society 21 Zetland Road, Redland, Bristol BS6 7AH. *Tel.* 0117 9427419.

Cancer Relief Macmillan Fund Anchor House, 15–18 Britten Street, London SW3 3TZ. *Tel.* 0171 351 7811; *Fax* 0171 376 8098.

Cancerlink 17 Brittania Street, London WC1X 9JN. *Tel.* Cancer Information Service 0171 833 2451; Asian Language Line 0171 713 7867; MAC helpline for young people affected by cancer: Freephone 0800 591028.

Carers National Association Ruth Pitter House, 20/25 Glasshouse Yard, London EC1A 4JS. *Tel.* 0171 490 8818; *Fax* 0171 490 8824.

CHAR 5–15 Cromer Street, London WC1H 8LS. *Tel.* 0171 833 2071.

Child Poverty Action Group 4th Floor, 1–5 Bath Street, London EC1V 9PY. *Tel.* 0171 253 3406.

Children's Legal Centre, The University of Essex, Wivenhoe Park, Colchester, Essex CO4 3SQ. *Tel.* 01206 873820.

CITA (Council for Involuntary Tranquilliser Addiction) Cavendish House, Brighton Road, Waterloo, Liverpool L22 5NG. Helpline: 0151 949 0102; Business Line: 0151 474 9626.

Citizen's Charter Publication Line Apex House, London Road, Bracknell, Berkshire RG12 2XH. *Tel.* 0345 223242; *Fax* 01344 360899.

Civil Aviation Authority Greville House, 37 Gratton Road, Cheltenham, Gloucestershire GL50 2BN. *Tel.* 01242 235151; *Fax* 01242 584139.

Commission for Racial Equality (CRE) Elliott House, 10/12 Allington Street, London SW1E 5EH. *Tel.* 0171 828 7022.

Community Self-Build Agency, The 40 Bowling Green Lane, London EC1R 0NE. *Tel.* 0171 415 7092.

Community Transport Association Highbank, Halton Street, Hyde, Cheshire SK14 2NY. *Tel./Fax* 0161 366 6685.

Counsel and Care Twyman House, 16 Bonny Street, London NW1 9PG. *Tel.* 0171 485 1566.

Council for Complementary and Alternative Medicine Suite D, Park House, 206–208 Latimer Road, London W10 6RE. *Tel.* 0181 968 3862; *Fax* 0181 968 3469.

Council Tenant's Charter, The FREEPOST, Dept 7DT, Newcastle-upon-Tyne NE85 1BR.

Cruse – Bereavement Care 126 Sheen Road, Richmond TW9 1UR. *Tel.* 0181 940 4818; Helpline: 0181 332 7227.

D*a*RT Dial-a-Ride and Taxicard Users   St Margarets, 25 Leighton Road, London NW5 2QD. *Tel.* 0171 482 2325; *Fax* 0171 284 2081.

Department for Education and Employment   Sanctuary Building, Great Smith Street, London SW1 P3BT. *Tel.* 0171 925 5555. *or* Department for Education and Employment   PO Box 6927, London E3 EN2. *Tel.* 0171 510 0150.

Department of the Environment   FREEPOST, PO Box 151, London E15 2HF.

Department of Health   PO Box 410, Wetherby, West Yorkshire LS23 7LN. *Tel.* 01937 840250; *Fax* 0990 210 266; Leaflet Line: 0800 555 777.

Department of Transport Mobility Unit   Room S10/20, 2 Marsham Street, London SW1P 3EB.

Depressives Anonymous   36 Chestnut Avenue, Beverley, North Humberside HU17 9QU. *Tel.* 01482 860619.

DIAL UK   St Catherine's Hospital, Park Lodge, Tickhill Road, Balby, Doncaster DN4 8QN. *Tel.* 01302 310123.

Disability Alliance   Universal House, 88–94 Wentworth House, London E1 7SA. *Tel.* 0171 247 8776; *Fax* 0171 247 8765.

Disabled Living Foundation   380–384 Harrow Road, London W9 2HU. *Tel.* 0171 289 6111; *Fax* 0171 266 2922.

Educational Counselling and Credit Transfer Information Service (ECCTIS)   ECCTIS 2000 Ltd, Fulton House, Jessop Avenue, Cheltenham, Gloucestershire. *Tel.* 01242 518724.

Employment Service   Rockingham House, 123 West Street, Sheffield S1 4ER. *Tel.* 0114 273 9190; *Fax* 0114 259 6496.

Family Fund   PO Box 50, York YO1 2ZX. *Tel.* 01904 621115.

Family Planning Association   27–35 Mortimer Street, London W1N 7RJ. *Tel.* 0171 636 7866.

Family Policy Studies Centre   231 Baker Street, London NW1 6XE. *Tel.* 0171 486 7680.

Family Rights Group   The Print House, 18 Ashwin Street, London E8 3DL. *Tel.* 0171 923 2628.

General Council and Register of Osteopaths   56 London Street, Reading, Berkshire RG1 4SQ. *Tel.* 01734 576585; *Fax* 01734 566246.

General Dental Council   37 Wimpole Street, London W1M 8DQ. *Tel.* 0171 486 2171; *Fax* 0171 224 3294.

Health Education Authority   Hamilton House, Mabledon Place, London WC1H 9TX.

HMSO Oldham   The Causeway, Broadway Business Park, Broadgate, Chadderton, Oldham CL9 0JA.

Holiday Care Service   2nd Floor, Imperial Buildings, Victoria Road, Horley, Surrey RH6 7PZ. *Tel.* 01293 774535; *Fax* 01293 784647.

Horticultural Therapy   Goulds Ground, Vallis Way, Frome, Somerset BA11 3DW. *Tel.* 01373 464782.

Hospice Information Service   St Christopher's Hospice, 51–59 Lawrie Park Road, Sydenham, London SE26 6OZ. *Tel.* 0181 778 9252; *Fax* 0181 776 9345.

Housing Association Tenants' Ombudsman Service   Palladium House, 1–4 Argyle Street, London W1V 1AD. *Tel.* 0171 437 1422.

Housing Corporation, The   149 Tottenham Court Road, London W1P 0BN. *Tel.* 0171 393 2000.

Independent Living 93 Fund   PO Box 183, Nottingham NG8 3RD. *Tel.* 0115 942 8191; *Fax* 0115 929 3156.

Independent Schools Information Service (ISIS)   56 Buckingham Gate, London SW1E 6AG. *Tel.* 0171 630 8793.

Institute for Complementary Medicine   Unit 15, Tavern Quay, Commercial Centre, Rope Street, London SE16 1TX.

Institute for the Study of Drug Dependence, The (ISDD)   1 Hatton Place, London EC1N 8ND. *Tel.* 0171 430 1991.

International Federation of Aromatherapists   Stamford House, 2–4 Chiswick High Road, London W4 1TH. *Tel.* 0181 742 2605.

International Society of Professional Aromatherapists   The Annexe, Hinckley and District Hospital, Hinckley, Leicestershire LE10 1AG. *Tel.* 01455 637987.

Kings Fund, The   11–13 Cavendish Square, London W1M 0AN. *Tel.* 0171 307 2400.

London Lighthouse   111/117 Lancaster Road, London W11 1QT. *Tel.* 0171 792 1200.

London Regional Transport Unit for Disabled Passengers   Brittania House, 1–11 Glenthorne Road, Hammersmith, London W6 0LF. *Tel.* 0181 748 7272.

London Transport Unit for Disabled Passengers   172 Buckingham Palace Road, London SW1W 9TN. *Tel.* 0171 918 3312; *Fax* 0171 918 3876.

Maric Curie Cancer Care   28 Belgrave Square, London SW1X 8QG. *Tel.* 0171 235 3325.

Marie Stopes International   108 Whitfield Street, London W1P 6BE. *Tel.* 0171 388 0662; *Fax* 0171 383 7196.

Medical Advisory Service, The   38 Sutton Court Road, London W4 4NJ. *Tel.* 0181 995 8503; *Fax* 0181 995 3275.

MENCAP   123 Golden Lane, London EC1Y 0RT.   *Tel.* 0171 696 5569; *Fax* 0171 607 3254.

MIND The Mental Health Charity   15–19 Broadway, London E15 4BQ. *Tel.* 0181 519 2122; *Fax* 0181 522 1725.

Mobility Advice and Vehicle Information Service (MAVIS)   Department of Transport, TRL, Crowthorne, Berkshire RG45 6AU. *Tel.* 01344 770456.

Mobility Information Service (MIS)   National Mobility Centre, Unit 2a, Atcham Industrial Estate, Shrewsbury SY4 4UG. *Tel.* 01743 761889.

Motability   Goodman House, Station Approach, Harlow, Essex CM20 2ET. *Tel.* 01279 635666.

NAM Publications Ltd   52 The Eurolink Centre, 49 Effra Road, London SW2 1BZ. *Tel.* 0171 737 1846.

Narcotics Anonymous   UK Service Office, PO Box 1980, London N19 3LS. *Tel.* 0171 351 6794.

National Association of Health Authorities and Trusts   Birmingham Research Park, Vincent Drive, Birmingham B15 2SQ.   *Tel.* 0121 471 4444; *Fax* 0121 414 1120.

National Childminding Association   8 Masons Hill, Bromley, Kent BR2 9EY. *Tel.* 0181 464 6164; *Fax* 0181 290 6834.

National Children's Bureau   8 Wakely Street, London EC1V 7QE. *Tel.* 0171 843 6000.

National Federation of Housing Associations   175 Gray's Inn Road, London WC1X 8UP. *Tel.* 0171 278 6571; *Fax* 0171 955 5696.

National House Building Council (NHBC)   Buildmark House, Chiltern Avenue, Amersham, Bucks HP6 5AP. *Tel.* 01494 434477.

National Institute for Medical Herbalists   56 Longbrook Street, Exeter EX4 6AH. *Tel.* 01392 426022.

National Schizophrenia Fellowship   28 Castle Street, Kingston upon Thames, Surrey KT1 1SS. *Tel.* 0181 547 3937.

National Society for the Prevention of Cruelty to Children (NSPCC)   National Centre, 42 Curtain Road, London EC2A 3NH. *Tel.* 0171 825 2500.

NCH Action for Children   85 Highbury Park, London N5 1UD. *Tel.* 0171 226 2033.

Open College, The   St Paul's, 781 Wilmslow Road, Didsbury, Manchester M20 2RW. *Tel.* 0161 434 0007; *Fax* 0161 434 1061.

Open University, The   Central Enquiry Service, PO Box 200, Milton Keynes MK7 6YZ.

Patients Association, The 8 Guildford Street, London WC1N 1DT. *Tel.* 0171 242 3460; *Fax* 0171 242 3461.
Patient's Charter and You, The   FREEPOST, London SE99 7XU.
Patient's Charter Unit   NHS Executive HQ, 4N34B Quarry House, Quarry Hill, Leeds LS2 7UE.
People First Instrument House, 207–215 Kings Cross Road, London WC1X 9DB. *Tel./Fax* 0171 713 6400.
Positively Women   347–349 City Road, London EC1V 1LR. *Tel.* 0171 713 0222; *Fax* 0171 713 1020.
Pregnancy Advisory Service 11–13 Charlotte Street, London W1P 1HD. *Tel.* 0171 637 8962 *and* Rosslyn Clinic, 15 Rosslyn Road, East Twickenham, Middlesex TW1 2AR. *Tel.* 0181 891 3173.
Pre-School Learning Alliance 60 Kings Cross Road, London WC1X 9LL. *Tel.* 0171 833 0991; *Fax* 0171 837 4942.

RADAR (The Royal Association for Disability and Rehabilitation) 12 City Forum, 259 City Road, London EC1V 8AF. *Tel.* 0171 250 3222; *Fax* 0171 250 0212.
Register for Qualified Aromatherapists, The   23 Castle Street, Tiverton, Devon EX16 6RE. *Tel.* 01884 243172.
Re-solv (The Society for the Prevention of Solvent and Volatile Substance Abuse) 30A High Street, Stone, Staffordshire ST15 8AW. *Tel.* 01785 817885.
Resource Information Service   The Basement, 38 Great Pulteney Street, London EC1V 9JU. *Tel.* 0171 494 2408.
Richmond Fellowship 8 Addison Road, Kensington, London W14 8DL. *Tel.* 0171 603 6373; *Fax* 0171 602 8652.
Royal National Institute for the Blind (RNIB)   224 Great Portland Street, London W1N 6AA. *Tel.* 0171 388 1266.

SCODA (The Standing Conference on Drug Abuse)   1–4 Hatton Place, London EC1N 8ND. *Tel.* 0171 430 2341.
Shelter 88 Old Street, London EC1V 9HU. *Tel.* 0171 505 2000; *Fax* 0171 505 2169.
Shelter London 229–231 High Holburn, London WC1V 7DA. *Tel.* 0171 404 7447.
Sheltered Housing Advisory and Conciliation Service (SHACS)   Walkden House, 3–10 Melton Street, London NW1 2EJ. *Tel.* 0171 383 2006.
Sheltered Housing Services Ltd 8–9 Abbey Parade, London W5 1EE. *Tel.* 0181 997 9313.
Society of Chiropodists and Podiatrists, The   53 Welbeck Street, London W1M 7HE. *Tel.* 0171 486 3381; *Fax* 0171 935 6359.
Society of Homeopaths, The 2 Artizan Road, Northampton, NN1 4HU. *Tel.* 01604 21400; *Fax* 01604 22622.
STAT (The Society of Teachers of the Alexander Technique)   20 London House, 226 Fulham Road, London SW10 9EL. *Tel./Fax* 0171 352 1556.

Terrence Higgins Trust 52–54 Gray's Inn Road, London WC1X 8JU. *Tel.* 0171 831 0330; *Fax* 0171 242 0121.

Unemployment Unit   322 St John Street, London EC1V 4NT.

Young Minds Trust   2nd Floor, 102–108 Clerkenwell Road, London EC1M 5SA. *Tel.* 0171 336 8445.
Youthaid   322 St John Street, London EC1V 4NT.

Helplines

Adfam National   0171 638 3700.

Al-Anon Family Groups   Helpline 0171 403 0888.

Cancer Information Service   Freeline 0800 181199.

CITA (Council for Involuntary Tranquilliser Addiction)   Helpline 0151 949 0102.

Disability Alliance Rights Line   0171 247 8776.

Drinkline   0171 332 0202 from London *or* 0345 320202 from outside London.

Health Information Service   0800 665544.

Housing Advice Line   0171 404 6929.

Medical Advisory Service General Medical helpline   0181 994 9874.

National AIDS helpline   0800 567123;
  Arabic: 0800 282477, 6–10 Thursday;
  Bengali: 0800 371132, 6–10 Tuesday;
  Cantonese: 0800 282446, 6–10 Monday;
  Gujarati: 0800 371134, 6–10 Wednesday;
  Punjabi: 0800 371133, 6–10 Wednesday;
  Urdu: 0800 371135, 6–10 Wednesday;
  Welsh: 0800 371131, 10–2 daily.

National Drugs helpline   0800 776600.

Positively Women helpline   0171 490 2327.

The Terrence Higgins Trust helpline   0171 242 1010.

The Terrence Higgins Trust legal line   0171 405 2381.

Index